The Poetry of James Thomson

Volume III (of III) – Lyrical Pieces & Other Works

James Thomson was born in Ednam in Roxburghshire around 11th September 1700 and baptised on 15th September. He was the fourth of nine children to father Thomas, the Presbyterian minister of Ednam and mother Beatrix.

Apart from the exact date of his birth several other facts of his life cannot be verified.

It is thought Thomson may have attended the parish school of Southdean, his father having been appointed minster there a few months after the birth of his son, before attending the grammar school in Jedburgh in 1712. Accounts of his early abilities are almost always negative. Poetry however was his great love. In this he was encouraged by Robert Riccaltoun, a farmer, poet and Presbyterian minister; and Sir William Bennet, a whig laird who was also the patron of Allan Ramsay. Very few early poems by Thomson survive. It seems that on each New Year's Day he burned almost all of his year's output.

In the autumn of 1715 he entered the College of Edinburgh on a career path that would take him to the Presbyterian ministry. In college he studied metaphysics, Logic, Ethics, Greek, Latin and Natural Philosophy. He also became a member of the Grotesque Club, a literary group. Here he met his lifelong friend to be; David Mallet.

In 1716 his father, Thomas, died. Again, facts are hard to come by but there is a colourful local legend that he died whilst performing an exorcism.

In 1719 Thomson completed his arts course but rather than graduate he instead entered Divinity Hall to become a minister.

However Thomson was also keen on literary pursuits. He managed to obtain publication of several of his poems in the 'Edinburgh Miscellany'. With this as his calling card he followed Mallet to London in February 1725 in an attempt at further publishing success. For Thomson a career as a minister was now behind him.

In London, Thomson became a tutor to the son of Charles Hamilton, Lord Binning, via connections on his mother's side of the family. Through David Mallet, who by 1724 was now also a published poet, Thomson met the great English poets of the day including Richard Savage, Aaron Hill and Alexander Pope.

Beatrix, Thomson's mother died on 12th May 1725, around the time of his writing 'Winter', the first poem of 'The Seasons'. 'Winter' was first published by John Millian in 1726 with a second edition incorporating revisions, additions and a preface later that same year.

By 1727, Thomson was working on 'Summer', which he published in February, whilst working at Watt's Academy, a school for young gentlemen and a centre of Newtonian science.

That same year Millian published Thomson's 'A Poem to the Memory of Sir Isaac Newton' in memory of the great scientist who had passed in March.

Thomson now left Watt's academy hoping to further pursue his career. This was greatly helped by finding several patrons including Thomas Rundle, the countess of Hertford and Charles Talbot, 1st Baron Talbot.

Thomson worked hard to complete 'The Seasons' during the late 1720's. 'Spring' was completed in 1728 and finally Autumn in 1730. Now the complete set of four could be published together as 'The Seasons'.

During this period he also wrote other poems, as well as a play, his first, 'The Tragedy of Sophonisba' in 1729. The latter is best known today for its mention in Samuel Johnson's Lives of the English Poets, where Johnson records that one 'feeble' line of the poem – "O, Sophonisba, Sophonisba, O!" was parodied by the wags of the theatre as, "O, Jemmy Thomson, Jemmy Thomson, O!"

In 1730, he was appointed tutor to the son of Sir Charles Talbot, his patron and also Solicitor-General. Thomson would spend nearly two years with the young man on 'the grand tour' of Europe. On his return Talbot graciously arranged for Thomson to become a secretary in chancery, which gave him financial security during until Talbot's death in 1737. Meanwhile, in 1734 Thomson's major work 'Liberty' was published.

In 1740, he collaborated with Mallet on the masque 'Alfred' which was first performed at Cliveden, the country home of Frederick, Prince of Wales. Thomson's words for 'Rule Britannia', from that masque, and set to music by Thomas Arne, became one of the best-known British patriotic songs. The Prince settled on him a pension of £100 per annum. He also introduced him to George Lyttelton, who became his friend and patron.

In later years, Thomson lived in Richmond upon Thames, and it was there that he wrote his final work 'The Castle of Indolence', which was published just before his untimely death on 27th August 1748. Johnson writes on Thomson's death that "by taking cold on the water between London and Kew, he caught a disorder, which, with some careless exasperation, ended in a fever that put end to his life".

He was buried in St. Mary Magdalene church in Richmond.

Index of Poems
LYRICAL PIECES

Hymn on Solitude
A Nuptial Song
An Ode on Aeolus's Harp
MEMORIAL VERSES
On the Death of His Mother
To the Memory of Sir Isaac Newton
On the Death of Mr. William Aikman, the Painter
To the Memory of the Right Honourable the Lord Talbot
Epitaph on Miss Elizabeth Stanley
A Poem to the Memory of Mr. Congreve
EPISTLES
To Dodington: The Happy Man
To His Royal Highness the Prince of Wales
To the Rev. Patrick Murdoch
Lines Sent to George Lyttelton, Esq., Soon After the Death of His Wife
To Mrs. Mendez' Birthday
To the Incomparable Soporific Doctor
To Seraphina
To Amanda. I
To Amanda. II
To Amanda. III
MISCELLANEOUS POEMS
Britannia
A Paraphrase of the latter part of the sixth chapter of St. Matthew
On the report of a Wooden Bridge to be built at Westminster
A CHRONOLOGY TO ELUCIDATE THE LIFE AND TIMES OF THOMSON

LYRICAL PIECES

RULE, BRITANNIA!

This famous ode, which appeared in the last scene (Act II, Sc. V) of Alfred: A Masque, a dramatic piece in which Mallet collaborated with Thomson, was published in 1740.

When Britain first, at Heaven's command,
Arose from out the azure main,
This was the charter of the land,
And guardian angels sung this strain—
'Rule, Britannia, rule the waves;
Britons never will be slaves.'

The nations, not so blest as thee,
Must in their turns to tyrants fall;
While thou shalt flourish great and free,
The dread and envy of them all.
'Rule,' &c.

Still more majestic shalt thou rise,
More dreadful from each foreign stroke:
As the loud blast that tears the skies
Serves but to root thy native oak.
'Rule,' &c.

Thee haughty tyrants ne'er shall tame;
All their attempts to bend thee down
Will but arouse thy generous flame,
But work their woe and thy renown.
'Rule,' &c.

To thee belongs the rural reign;
Thy cities shall with commerce shine;
All thine shall be the subject main,
And every shore it circles thine.
'Rule,' &c.

The Muses, still with freedom found,
Shall to thy happy coast repair:
Blest isle! with matchless beauty crowned,
And manly hearts to guard the fair.
'Rule, Britannia, rule the waves;
Britons never will be slaves.'

ODE

Tell me, thou soul of her I love,
Ah! tell me, whither art thou fled?
To what delightful world above,
Appointed for the happy dead?

Or dost thou free at pleasure roam,
And sometimes share thy lover's woe
Where, void of thee, his cheerless home
Can now, alas! no comfort know?

Oh! if thou hoverest round my walk,
While, under every well-known tree,
I to thy fancied shadow talk,
And every tear is full of thee—

Should then the weary eye of grief
Beside some sympathetic stream
In slumber find a short relief,

Oh, visit thou my soothing dream!

[Cp. Burns's To Mary in Heaven.]

COME, GENTLE GOD

Come, gentle god of soft desire,
Come and possess my happy breast;
Not fury-like in flames and fire,
Or frantic folly's wildness drest.

But come in friendship's angel-guise;
Yet dearer thou than friendship art,
More tender spirit in thy eyes,
More sweet emotions at the heart.

O, come with goodness in thy train,
With peace and pleasure void of storm;
And, wouldst thou me for ever gain,
Put on Amanda's winning form.

SONG

One day the god of fond desire,
On mischief bent, to Damon said,
'Why not disclose your tender fire?
Not own it to the lovely maid?'

The shepherd marked his treacherous art,
And, softly sighing, thus replied:
"Tis true, you have subdued my heart,
But shall not triumph o'er my pride.

'The slave in private only bears
Your bondage, who his love conceals;
But, when his passion he declares,
You drag him at your chariot-wheels.'

SONG

Hard is the fate of him who loves
Yet dares not tell his trembling pain

But to the sympathetic groves,
But to the lonely listening plain.

Oh! when she blesses next your shade,
Oh! when her footsteps next are seen
In flowery tracts along the mead,
In fresher mazes o'er the green,

Ye gentle spirits of the vale,
To whom the tears of love are dear,
From dying lilies waft a gale
And sigh my sorrows in her ear.

Oh! tell her what she cannot blame,
Though fear my tongue must ever bind;
Oh! tell her that my virtuous flame
Is as her spotless soul refined.

Not her own guardian angel eyes
With chaster tenderness his care;
Not purer her own wishes rise,
Not holier her own sighs in prayer.

But, if at first her virgin fear
Should start at love's suspected name,
With that of friendship soothe her ear—
True love and friendship are the same.

TO AMANDA

Come, dear Amanda, quit the town,
And to the rural hamlets fly;
Behold! the wintry storms are gone,
A gentle radiance glads the sky;

The birds awake, the flowers appear,
Earth spreads a verdant couch for thee;
'Tis joy and music all we hear,
'Tis love and beauty all we see.

Come, let us mark the gradual spring,
How peeps the bud, the blossom blows;
Till Philomel begins to sing,
And perfect May to swell the rose.

Even so thy rising charms improve,

As life's warm season grows more bright;
And, opening to the sighs of love,
Thy beauties glow with full delight.

TO AMANDA

Unless with my Amanda blest,
In vain I twine the woodbine bower;
Unless to deck her sweeter breast,
In vain I rear the breathing flower.

Awakened by the genial year,
In vain the birds around me sing;
In vain the freshening fields appear:
Without my love there is no Spring.

TO MYRA

Myra is Amanda. The poem was enclosed in a letter to Mrs. Robertson (Amanda's sister), in 1742, and was first printed in the Earl of Buchan's Essay.

O thou whose tender serious eyes
Expressive speak the mind I love—
The gentle azure of the skies,
The pensive shadows of the grove

O mix their beauteous beams with mine,
And let us interchange our hearts;
Let all their sweetness on me shine,
Poured through my soul be all their darts.

Ah, 'tis too much! I cannot bear
At once so soft, so keen a ray:
In pity then, my lovely fair,
O turn those killing eyes away!

But what avails it to conceal
One charm where nought but charms I see?
Their lustre then again reveal,
And let me, Myra, die of thee!

TO FORTUNE

For ever, Fortune, wilt thou prove
An unrelenting foe to love,
And, when we meet a mutual heart,
Come in between and bid us part;

Bid us sigh on from day to day,
And wish, and wish the soul away;
Till youth and genial years are flown,
And all the life of life is gone?

But busy, busy still art thou,
To bind the loveless joyless vow,
The heart from pleasure to delude,
And join the gentle to the rude.

For once, O Fortune! hear my prayer,
And I absolve thy future care—
All other blessings I resign;
Make but the dear Amanda mine!

THE BASHFUL LOVER

From a MS. believed to be in Thomson's handwriting

Sweet tyrant Love, but hear me now!
And cure while young this pleasing smart;
Or rather, aid my trembling vow,
And teach me to reveal my heart.

Tell her whose goodness is my bane,
Whose looks have smiled my peace away,
Oh! whisper now she gives me pain,
Whilst undesigning, frank, and gay.

'Tis not for common charms I sigh,
For what the vulgar beauty call;
'Tis not a cheek, a lip, an eye;
But 'tis the soul that lights them all.

For that I drop the tender tear,
For that I make this artless moan,
Oh, sigh it, Love! into her ear,
And make the bashful lover known.

TO THE NIGHTINGALE

O Nightingale, best poet of the grove,
That plaintive strain can ne'er belong to thee.
Blest in the full possession of thy love:
O lend that strain, sweet nightingale, to me!

'Tis mine, alas! to mourn my wretched fate:
I love a maid who all my bosom charms,
Yet lose my days without this lovely mate;
Inhuman fortune keeps her from my arms.

You, happy birds! by nature's simple laws
Lead your soft lives, sustained by nature's fare;
You dwell wherever roving fancy draws,
And love and song is all your pleasing care:

But we, vain slaves of interest and of pride,
Dare not be blest lest envious tongues should blame:
And hence in vain I languish for my bride—
O mourn with me, sweet bird, my hapless flame.

HYMN ON SOLITUDE

Hail, mildly pleasing Solitude,
Companion of the wise and good;
But from whose holy piercing eye
The herd of fools and villains fly.
Oh! how I love with thee to walk,
And listen to thy whispered talk,
Which innocence and truth imparts,
And melts the most obdurate hearts.

A thousand shapes you wear with ease,
And still in every shape you please.
Now wrapt in some mysterious dream,
A lone philosopher you seem;
Now quick from hill to vale you fly,
And now you sweep the vaulted sky;
A shepherd next, you haunt the plain,
And warble forth your oaten strain;

A lover now, with all the grace
Of that sweet passion in your face;
Then, calmed to friendship, you assume

The gentle looking Harford's bloom,
As, with her Musidora, she
(Her Musidora fond of thee)
Amid the long-withdrawing vale
Awakes the rivalled nightingale.

Thine is the balmy breath of morn,
Just as the dew-bent rose is born;
And, while meridian fervours beat,
Thine is the woodland dumb retreat;
But chief, when evening scenes decay
And the faint landskip swims away,
Thine is the doubtful soft decline,
And that best hour of musing thine.

Descending angels bless thy train,
The virtues of the sage, and swain—
Plain Innocence in white arrayed
Before thee lifts her fearless head;
Religion's beams around thee shine
And cheer thy glooms with light divine;
About thee sports sweet Liberty;
And wrapt Urania sings to thee.

Oh, let me pierce thy secret cell,
And in thy deep recesses dwell!
Perhaps from Norwood's oak-clad hill,
When meditation has her fill,
I just may cast my careless eyes
Where London's spiry turrets rise,
Think of its crimes, its cares, its pain.
Then shield me in the woods again.

A NUPTIAL SONG

Intended to have been inserted in the fourth act of Sophonisba, Thomson's first play, acted at Drury Lane, February 28, 1730.

Come, gentle Venus! and assuage
A warring world, a bleeding age,
For nature lives beneath thy ray:
The wintry tempests haste away,
A lucid calm invests the sea,
Thy native deep is full of thee;
And flowering earth, where'er you fly,
Is all O' er spring, all sun the sky;

A genial spirit warms the breeze;
Unseen, among the blooming trees,
The feathered lovers tune their throat,
The desert growls a softened note,
Glad o'er the meads the cattle bound,
And love and harmony go round.

But chief into the human heart
You strike the dear delicious dart;
You teach us pleasing pangs to know,
To languish in luxurious woe,
To feel the generous passions rise,
Grow good by gazing, mild by sighs;
Each happy moment to improve,
And fill the perfect year with love.

Come, thou delight of heaven and earth!
To whom all creatures owe their birth;
Oh, come! red-smiling, tender, come!
And yet prevent our final doom.
For long the furious god of war
Has crushed us with his iron car,
Has raged along our ruined plains,
Has cursed them with his cruel stains,
Has sunk our youth in endless sleep,
And made the widowed virgin weep.
Now let him feel thy wonted charms,
Oh, take him to thy twining arms!
And, while thy bosom heaves on his,
While deep he prints the humid kiss,
Ah, then! his stormy heart control,
And sigh thyself into his soul.

Thy son too, Cupid, we implore
To leave the green Idalian shore.
Be he, sweet god! our only foe:
Long let him draw the twanging bow,
Transfix us with his golden darts,
Pour all his quiver on our hearts,
With gentler anguish make us sigh,
And teach us sweeter deaths to die.

AN ODE ON AEOLUS'S HARP

Ethereal race, inhabitants of air,
Who hymn your God amid the secret grove,

Ye unseen beings, to my harp repair,
And raise majestic strains, or melt in love.

Those tender notes, how kindly they upbraid!
With what soft woe they thrill the lover's heart!
Sure from the hand of some unhappy maid
Who died of love these sweet complainings part.

But hark! that strain was of a graver tone,
On the deep strings his hand some hermit throws;
Or he, the sacred Bard, who sat alone
In the drear waste and wept his people's woes.

Such was the song which Zion's children sung
When by Euphrates' stream they made their plaint;
And to such sadly solemn notes are strung
Angelic harps to soothe a dying saint.

Methinks I hear the full celestial choir
Through Heaven's high dome their awful anthem raise;
Now chanting clear, and now they all conspire
To swell the lofty hymn from praise to praise.

Let me, ye wandering spirits of the wind,
Who, as wild fancy prompts you, touch the string,
Smit with your theme, be in your chorus joined,
For till you cease my muse forgets to sing.

MEMORIAL VERSES ON THE DEATH OF HIS MOTHER

Written in 1725

Ye fabled muses, I your aid disclaim,
Your airy raptures, and your fancied flame:
True genuine woe my throbbing breast inspires,
Love prompts my lays, and filial duty fires;
The soul springs instant at the warm design
And the heart dictates every flowing line.

See! where the kindest, best of mothers lies,
And death has shut her ever weeping eyes;
Has lodged at last in peace her weary breast,
And lulled her many piercing cares to rest.
No more the orphan train around her stands,
While her full heart upbraids her needy hands!
No more the widow's lonely fate she feels,

The shock severe that modest wants conceals,
The oppressor's scourge, the scorn of wealthy pride,
And poverty's unnumbered ills beside.
For see! attended by the angelic throng,
Through yonder worlds of light she glides along,
And claims the well-earned raptures of the sky.
Yet fond concern recalls the mother's eye;
She seeks the helpless orphans left behind—
So hardly left! so bitterly resigned!
Still, still is she my soul's divinest theme,
The waking vision, and the wailing dream:
Amid the ruddy sun's enlivening blaze
O'er my dark eyes her dewy image plays,
And in the dread dominion of the night
Shines out again the sadly pleasing sight.
Triumphant virtue all around her darts.
And more than volumes every look imparts—
Looks soft, yet awful; melting, yet serene;
Where both the mother and the saint are seen.
But ah! that night, that torturing night remains—
May darkness dye it with its deepest stains,
May joy on it forsake her rosy bowers,
And screaming sorrow blast its baleful hours!
When on the margin of the briny flood,
Chilled with a sad presaging damp I stood,
Took the last look, ne'er to behold her more,
And mixed our murmurs with the wavy roar,
Heard the last words fall from her pious tongue.
Then wild into the bulging vessel flung—
Which soon, too soon, conveyed me from her sight,
Dearer than life, and liberty, and light!
Why was I then, ye powers, reserved for this,
Nor sunk that moment in the vast abyss?
Devoured at once by the relentless wave,
And whelmed for ever in a watery grave?
Down, ye wild wishes of unruly woe!
I see her with immortal beauty glow;
The early wrinkle, care-contracted, gone,
Her tears all wiped, and all her sorrows flown;
The exalting voice of Heaven I hear her breathe,
To soothe her soul in agonies of death.
I see her through the mansions blest above,
And now she meets her dear expecting love.
Heart-cheering sight! but yet, alas! o'erspread
By the damp gloom of grief's uncheerful shade.
Come, then, of reason the reflecting hour,
And let me trust the kind o'erruling power
Who from the night commands the shining day,

The poor man's portion, and the orphan's stay.

TO THE MEMORY OF SIR ISAAC NEWTON

Written in 1727

Shall the great soul of Newton quit this earth
To mingle with his stars, and every Muse,
Astonished into silence, shun the weight
Of honours due to his illustrious name?
But what can man? Even now the sons of light,
In strains high warbled to seraphic lyre,
Hail his arrival on the coast of bliss.
Yet am not I deterred, though high the theme,
And sung to harps of angels, for with you,
Ethereal Hames! ambitious, I aspire
In Nature's general symphony to join.

And what new wonders can ye show your guest!
Who, while on this dim spot where mortals toil
Clouded in dust, from motion's simple laws
Could trace the secret hand of Providence,
Wide-working through this universal frame.

Have ye not listened while he bound the suns
And planets to their spheres! the unequal task
Of humankind till then. Oft had they rolled
O'er erring man the year, and oft disgraced
The pride of schools, before their course was known
Full in its causes and effects to him,
All-piercing sage! who sat not down and dreamed
Romantic schemes, defended by the din
Of specious words, and tyranny of names;
But, bidding his amazing mind attend,
And with heroic patience years on years
Deep-searching, saw at last the system dawn,
And shine, of all his race, on him alone.

What were his raptures then! how pure! how strong!
And what the triumphs of old Greece and Rome,
By his diminished, but the pride of boys
In some small fray victorious! when instead
Of shattered parcels of this earth usurped
By violence unmanly, and sore deeds
Of cruelty and blood, Nature herself
Stood all subdued by him, and open laid

Her every latent glory to his view.

All intellectual eye, our solar round
First gazing through, he, by the blended power
Of gravitation and projection, saw
The whole in silent harmony revolve.
From unassisted vision hid, the moons
To cheer remoter planets numerous formed,
By him in all their mingled tracts were seen.
He also fixed our wandering Queen of Night,
Whether she wanes into a scanty orb,
Or, waxing broad, with her pale shadowy light,
In a soft deluge overflows the sky.
Her every motion clear-discerning, he
Adjusted to the mutual main and taught
Why now the mighty mass of waters swells
Resistless, heaving on the broken rocks,
And the full river turning—till again
The tide revertive, unattracted, leaves
A yellow waste of idle sands behind.

Then, breaking hence, he took his ardent flight
Through the blue infinite; and every star,
Which the clear concave of a winter's night
Pours on the eye, or astronomic tube,
Far stretching, snatches from the dark abyss,
Or such as further in successive skies
To fancy shine alone, at his approach
Blazed into suns, the living centre each
Of an harmonious system—all combined,
And ruled unerring by that single power
Which draws the stone projected to the ground.

O unprofuse magnificence divine!
O wisdom truly perfect! thus to call
From a few causes such a scheme of things,
Effects so various, beautiful, and great,
An universe complete! And O beloved
Of Heaven! whose well purged penetrating eye
The mystic veil transpiercing, inly scanned
The rising, moving, wide-established frame.

He, first of men, with awful wing pursued
The comet through the long elliptic curve,
As round innumerous worlds he wound his way,
Till, to the forehead of our evening sky
Returned, the blazing wonder glares anew,
And o'er the trembling nations shakes dismay.

The heavens are all his own, from the wide rule
Of whirling vortices and circling spheres
To their first great simplicity restored.
The schools astonished stood; but found it vain
To combat still with demonstration strong,
And, unawakened, dream beneath the blaze
Of truth. At once their pleasing visions fled,
With the gay shadows of the morning mixed,
When Newton rose, our philosophic sun!

The aerial flow of sound was known to him,
From whence it first in wavy circles breaks,
Till the touched organ takes the message in.
Nor could the darting beam of speed immense
Escape his swift pursuit and measuring eye.
Even Light itself, which every thing displays,
Shone undiscovered, till his brighter mind
Untwisted all the shining robe of day;
And, from the whitening undistinguished blaze,
Collecting every ray into his kind,
To the charmed eye educed the gorgeous train
Of parent colours. First the flaming red
Sprung vivid forth; the tawny orange next;
And next delicious yellow; by whose side
Fell the kind beams of all-refreshing green.
Then the pure blue, that swells autumnal skies,
Ethereal played; and then, of sadder hue,
Emerged the deepened indigo, as when
The heavy-skirted evening droops with frost;
While the last gleamings of refracted light
Died in the fainting violet away.
These, when the clouds distil the rosy shower,
Shine out distinct adown the watery bow;
While o'er our heads the dewy vision bends
Delightful, melting on the fields beneath.
Myriads of mingling dyes from these result,
And myriads still remain—infinite source
Of beauty, ever flushing, ever new.

Did ever poet image aught so fair,
Dreaming in whispering groves by the hoarse brook?
Or prophet, to whose rapture heaven descends?
Even now the setting sun and shifting clouds,
Seen, Greenwich, from thy lovely heights, declare
How just, how beauteous the refractive law.

The noiseless tide of time, all bearing down

To vast eternity's unbounded sea,
Where the green islands of the happy shine,
He stemmed alone; and, to the source (involved
Deep in primeval gloom) ascending, raised
His lights at equal distances, to guide
Historian wildered on his darksome way.

But who can number up his labours? who
His high discoveries sing? When but a few
Of the deep-studying race can stretch their minds
To what he knew—in fancy's lighter thought
How shall the muse then grasp the mighty theme?

What wonder thence that his devotion swelled
Responsive to his knowledge? For could he
Whose piercing mental eye diffusive saw
The finished university of things
In all its order, magnitude, and parts
Forbear incessant to adore that Power
Who fills, sustains, and actuates the whole?

Say, ye who best can tell, ye happy few,
Who saw him in the softest lights of life,
All unwithheld, indulging to his friends
The vast unborrowed treasures of his mind,
Oh, speak the wondrous man! how mild, how calm,
How greatly humble, how divinely good,
How firmly stablished on eternal truth;
Fervent in doing well, with every nerve
Still pressing on, forgetful of the past,
And panting for perfection; far above
Those little cares and visionary joys
That so perplex the fond impassioned heart
Of ever cheated, ever trusting man.
This, Conduitt, from thy rural hours we hope,
As through the pleasing shade where nature pours
Her every sweet in studious ease you walk,
The social passions smiling at thy heart
That glows with all the recollected sage.

And you, ye hopeless gloomy-minded tribe,
You who, unconscious of those nobler flights
That reach impatient at immortal life,
Against the prime endearing privilege
Of being dare contend,—say, can a soul
Of such extensive, deep, tremendous powers,
Enlarging still, be but a finer breath
Of spirits dancing through their tubes awhile,

And then for ever lost in vacant air?

But hark! methinks I hear a warning voice,
Solemn as when some awful change is come,
Sound through the world—"Tis done!—the measure's full;
And I resign my charge.'—Ye mouldering stones
That build the towering pyramid, the proud
Triumphal arch, the monument effaced
By ruthless ruin, and whate'er supports
The worshipped name of hoar antiquity—
Down to the dust! What grandeur can ye boast
While Newton lifts his column to the skies,
Beyond the waste of time. Let no weak drop
Be shed for him. The virgin in her bloom
Cut off, the joyous youth, and darling child—
These are the tombs that claim the tender tear
And elegiac song. But Newton calls
For other notes of gratulation high,
That now he wanders through those endless worlds
He here so well descried, and wondering talks,
And hymns their Author with his glad compeers.
O Britain's boast! whether with angels thou
Sittest in dread discourse, or fellow-blessed,
Who joy to see the honour of their kind;
Or whether, mounted on cherubic wing,
Thy swift career is with the whirling orbs,
Comparing things with things, in rapture lost,
And grateful adoration for that light
So plenteous rayed into thy mind below
From Light Himself; oh, look with pity down
On humankind, a frail erroneous race!
Exalt the spirit of a downward world!
O'er thy dejected country chief preside,
And be her Genius called! her studies raise,
Correct her manners, and inspire her youth;
For, though depraved and sunk, she brought thee forth,
And glories in thy name! she points thee out
To all her sons, and bids them eye thy star:
While, in expectance of the second life
When time shall be no more, thy sacred dust
Sleeps with her kings, and dignifies the scene.

ON THE DEATH OF MR. WILLIAM AIKMAN, THE PAINTER

Oh, could I draw, my friend, thy genuine mind
Just as the living forms by thee designed,

Of Raphael's figures none should fairer shine,
Nor Titian's colours longer last than mine.
A mind in wisdom old, in lenience young,
From fervent truth where every virtue sprung;
Where all was real, modest, plain, sincere;
Worth above show, and goodness unsevere:
Viewed round and round, as lucid diamonds throw
Still as you turn them a revolving glow,
So did his mind reflect with secret ray
In various virtues heaven's internal day;
Whether in high discourse it soared sublime
And sprung impatient o'er the bounds of time,
Or, wandering nature through with raptured eye,
Adored the hand that turned yon azure sky:
Whether to social life he bent his thought,
And the right poise of mingling passions sought,
Gay converse blest; or in the thoughtful grove
Bid the heart open every source of love:
New varying lights still set before your eyes
The just, the good, the social, or the wise.
For such a death who can, who would refuse
The friend a tear, a verse the mournful muse?

Yet pay we just acknowledgement to heaven,
Though snatched so soon, that Aikman e'er was given.
A friend, when dead, is but removed from sight,
Hid in the lustre of eternal light:
Oft with the mind he wonted converse keeps
In the lone walk, or when the body sleeps
Lets in a wandering ray, and all elate
Wings and attracts her to another state;
And, when the parting storms of life are o'er,
May yet rejoin him in a happier shore.

As those we love decay, we die in part,
String after string is severed from the heart;
Till loosened life, at last but breathing clay,
Without one pang is glad to fall away.
Unhappy he who latest feels the blow,
Whose eyes have wept o'er every friend laid low,
Dragged lingering on from partial death to death,
Till, dying, all he can resign is breath.

TO THE MEMORY OF THE RIGHT HONOURABLE THE LORD TALBOT, LATE CHANCELLOR OF GREAT BRITAIN

First printed in June, 1737, with a dedication to the Rt. Hon. the Lord Talbot

While with the public, you, my Lord, lament
A friend and father lost; permit the muse,
The muse assigned of old a double theme,
To praise dead worth and humble living pride,
Whose generous task begins where interest ends;
Permit her on a Talbot's tomb to lay
This cordial verse sincere, by truth inspired,
Which means not to bestow but borrow fame.
Yes, she may sing his matchless virtues now—
Unhappy that she may! But where begin!
How from the diamond single out each ray,
That, though they tremble with ten thousand hues,
Effuse one poignant undivided light?

Let the low-minded of these narrow days
No more presume to deem the lofty tale
Of ancient times, in pity to their own,
Romance. In Talbot we united saw
The piercing eye, the quick enlightened soul,
The graceful ease, the flowing tongue of Greece,
Joined to the virtues and the force of Rome.

Eternal Wisdom, that all-quickening sun,
Whence every life in just proportion draws
Directing light and actuating flame,
Ne'er with a larger portion of its beams
Awakened mortal clay. Hence steady, calm,
Diffusive, deep, and clear his reason saw
With instantaneous view the truth of things;
Chief what to human life and human bliss
Pertains, that kindest science, fit for man:
And hence, responsive to his knowledge, glowed
His ardent virtue. Ignorance and vice
In consort foul agree, each heightening each;
While virtue draws from knowledge nobler fire,
Is knowledge of true pleasure, proved by deeds.

What grand, what comely, and what tender sense.
What talent, and what virtue was not his?
All that can render man or great or good,
Give useful worth, or amiable grace?
Nor could he brook in studious shade to lie
In soft retirement indolently pleased
With selfish peace. The Syren of the wise
(Who steals the Aonian song, and in the shape
Of Virtue woos them from a worthless world)
Though deep he felt her charms, could never melt

His strenuous spirit, recollected, calm
As silent night, yet active as the day.
The more the bold, the bustling, and the bad
Usurp the reins of power, the more behoves,
Becomes it virtue with indignant zeal
To' check their conjuration. Shall low views
Of sneaking interest or luxurious vice,
'The villain's passions, quicken more to toil,
And dart a livelier vigour through the soul,
Than those that, mingled with our truest good.
With present honour and immortal fame,
Involve the good of all? An empty form,
Vain is the virtue that amid the shade
Lamenting lies, with future schemes amused,
While wickedness and folly, kindred powers,
Confound the world. A Talbot's, different far,
Sprung into action—action; that disdained
To lose in living death one pulse of life,
That might be saved; disdained, for coward ease
And her insipid pleasures, to resign
The prize of glory, the keen sweets of toil,
And those high joys that teach the truly great
To live for others, and for others die.

Early, behold! he breaks benign on life.
Not breathing more beneficence, the spring
Leads in her swelling train the gentle airs:
While gay behind her smiles the kindling waste
Of ruffian storms and Winter's lawless rage.
In him Astrea, to this dim abode
Of ever-wandering men, returned again—
To bless them his delight, to bring them back
From thorny error, from unjoyous wrong,
Into the paths of kind primeval faith,
Of happiness and justice. All his parts,
His virtues all collected sought the good
Of humankind. For that he fervent felt
The throb of patriots, when they model states:
Anxious for that, nor needful sleep could hold
His still-awakened soul; nor friends had charms
To steal with pleasing guile an healing hour;
Toil knew no languor, no attraction joy.
The common father such of erring men!
A froward race! incessant in pursuit
Of flying good or of fallacious bliss;
Still as they thwart and mingle in the chace,
Now fraud, now force, now cruelty and crimes,
Attempting all to seize a brother's prize;

He sits superior to the little fray,
Detects the legal snares of mazy guile,
With the proud mighty bids the feeble cope,
And into social life the villain daunts.
Be named, victorious ravagers, no more!
Vanish, ye human comets! shrink your blaze!
Ye that your glory to your terrors owe,
As, o'er the gazing desolated earth,
You scatter famine, pestilence, and war;
Vanish! before this vernal sun of fame,
Effulgent sweetness! beaming life and joy.

How the heart listened while he pleading spoke!
While on the enlightened mind, with winning art,
His gentle reason so persuasive stole
That the charmed hearer thought it was his own.
Ah! when, ye studious of the laws, again
Shall such enchanting lessons bless your ear?
When shall again the darkest truths, perplexed,
Be set in ample day? Again the harsh
And arduous open into smiling ease?
The solid mix with elegant delight?
To him the purest eloquence indulged
Eternal treasure, light and heat combined,
At once to pour conviction on the soul,
And mould with lawful flame the impassioned heart.
That dangerous gift, which to the strictly just
And good alone belongs, lay safe with him
Reposed. He sacred to his country's cause,
To trampled want and worth, to suffering right,
To the lone widow's and her orphan's woes,
Reserved the mighty charm. With equal brow,
Despising then the smiles or frowns of power,
He all that noblest eloquence effused
Which wakes the tender or exalting tear,
When generous passions, taught by reason, speak.
Then spoke the man, and over barren art
Prevailed abundant nature. Freedom then
His client was, humanity and truth.

Placed on the seat of justice, there he reigned
In a superior sphere of cloudless day,
A pure intelligence. No tumult there,
No dark emotion, no intemperate heat,
No passion e'er disturbed the clear serene
That round him spread. A zeal for right alone,
The love of justice, like the steady sun
Unbating ardour lent; and now and then,

Against the sons of violence, of pride,
And bold deceit his indignation gleamed.
As intuition quick, he snatched the truth,
Yet with progressive patience, step by step,
Self-diffident, or to the slower kind,
He through the maze of falsehood traced it on,
Till, at the last evolved, it full appeared,
And e'en the loser owned the just decree.

But, when in senates he, to freedom firm,
Enlightened freedom, planned salubrious laws,
His various learning, his wide knowledge then
His insight deep into Britannia's weal,
Spontaneous seemed from simple sense to flow,
And the plain patriot smoothed the brow of law.
No specious swell, no frothy pomp of words
Fell on the cheated ear; no studied maze
Of declamation to perplex the right
He darkening threw around: safe in itself,
In its own force, almighty Reason spoke;
While on the great, the ruling point, at once
He streamed decisive day, and showed it vain
To lengthen farther out the clear debate.
Conviction breathes conviction; to the heart,
Poured ardent forth in eloquence unbid,
The heart attends: for, let the venal try
Their every hardening stupefying art,
Truth must prevail, zeal will enkindle zeal,
And Nature, skilful touched, is honest still.

Behold him in the councils of his prince.
What faithful light he lends! How rare in courts
Such wisdom! such abilities! and, joined
To virtue so determined, public zeal,
And honour of such adamantine proof
As even corruption, hopeless and o'erawed,
Durst not have tempted! Yet of manners mild,
And winning every heart, he knew to please,
Nobly to please; while equally he scorned
Or adulation to receive or give.
Happy the state where wakes a ruling eye
Of such inspection keen and general care
Beneath a guard so vigilant, so pure,
All-trusted, all-revered, and all-beloved,
Toil may resign his careless head to rest,
And ever-jealous freedom sleep in peace.
Ah! lost untimely! lost in downward days!
And many a patriot counsel with him lost!

Counsels, that might have humbled Britain's foe,
Her native foe, from eldest time by fate
Appointed, as did once a Talbot's arms.

Let learning, arts, let universal worth
Lament a patron lost, a friend and judge—
Unlike the sons of vanity, that, veiled
Beneath the patron's prostituted name,
Dare sacrifice a worthy man to pride,
And flush confusion o'er an honest cheek.
Obliged when he obliged, it seemed a debt
Which he to merit, to the public, paid,
That can alone by virtue stationed high
Recover fame; to his own heart a debt,
And to the great all-bounteous Source of good!
The gracious flood that cheers the lettered world
Is not the noisy gift of summer's noon,
Whose sudden current from the naked root
Washes the little soil which yet remained,
And only more dejects the blushing flowers:
No, 'tis the soft-descending dews at eve,
The silent treasures of the vernal year
Indulging deep their stores the still night long—
Till with returning morn the freshened world
Is fragrance all, all beauty, joy, and song.

Still let me view him in the pleasing light
Of private life, where pomp forgets to glare,
And where the plain unguarded soul is seen.
Not only there most amiable, best,
But with that truest greatness he appeared,
Which thinks not of appearing; kindly veiled
In the soft graces of the friendly scene,
Inspiring social confidence and ease.
As free the converse of the wise and good,
As joyous, disentangling every power,
And breathing mixed improvement with delight,
As when amid the various-blossomed spring,
Or gentle beaming autumn's pensive shade,
The philosophic mind with nature talks.
Say ye, his sons, his dear remains, with whom
The father laid superfluous state aside,
Yet swelled your filial duty thence the more,
With friendship swelled it, with esteem, with love,
Beyond the ties of blood, oh! speak the joy,
The pure serene, the cheerful wisdom mild,
The virtuous spirit, which his vacant hours
In semblance of amusement through the breast

Infused. And thou, O Rundle! lend thy strain,
Thou darling friend! thou brother of his soul!
In whom the head and heart their stores unite—
Whatever fancy paints, invention pours,
Judgement digests, the well-tuned bosom feels,
Truth natural, moral, or divine has taught,
The virtues dictate, or the Muses sing.
Lend me the plaint, which, to the lonely main.
With memory conversing, you will pour,
As on the pebbled shore you pensive stray
Where Derry's mountains a bleak crescent form,
And mid their ample round receive the waves
That from the frozen pole, resounding, rush
Impetuous. Though from native sunshine driven,
Driven from your friends, the sunshine of the soul,
By slanderous zeal and politics infirm,
Jealous of worth; yet will you bless your lot,
Yet will you triumph in your glorious fate,
Whence Talbot's friendship glows to future times,
Intrepid, warm; of kindred tempers born
Nursed by experience into slow esteem,
Calm confidence unbounded love not blind,
And the sweet light from mingled minds disclosed,
From mingled chymic oils as bursts the fire.

I too remember well that mental bowl
Which round his table flowed. The serious there
Mixed with the sportive, with the learned the plain;
Mirth softened wisdom, candour tempered mirth,
And wit its honey lent without the sting.
Not simple nature's unaffected sons,
The blameless Indians, round their forest cheer,
In sunny lawn or shady covert set,
Hold more unspotted converse; nor, of old,
Rome's awful consuls, her dictator-swains,
As on the product of their Sabine farms
They fared, with stricter virtue fed the soul:
Nor yet in Athens, at an Attic meal,
Where Socrates presided, fairer truth,
More elegant humanity, more grace,
Wit more refined, or deeper science reigned.
But far beyond the little vulgar bounds
Of family, of friends, of country kind,
By just degrees and with proportioned flame
Extended his benevolence: a friend
To humankind, to parent nature's works.
Of free access, and of engaging grace,
Such as a brother to a brother owes,

He kept an open judging ear for all,
And spread an open countenance where smiled
The fair effulgence of an open heart;
While on the rich, the poor, the high, the low
With equal ray his ready goodness shone:
For nothing human foreign was to him.

Thus to a dread inheritance, my Lord,
And hard to be supported, you succeed:
But, kept by virtue, as by virtue gained,
It will through latest time enrich your race,
When grosser wealth shall moulder into dust,
And with their authors in oblivion sunk
Vain titles lie, the, servile badges oft
Of mean submission, not the meed of worth
True genuine honour its large patent holds
Of all mankind, through every land and age,
Of universal reason's various sons,
And even of God himself, sole perfect Judge!
Who sees with other eyes than flattering men.
Meantime these noblest honours of the mind
On rigid terms descend: the high-placed heir,
Scanned by the public eye, that with keen gaze
Malignant seeks out faults, cannot through life
Amid the nameless insects of a court,
If such to life belong, unheeded steal:
He must be glorious, or he must be base.
This truth to you, who merit well to bear
A name to Britons dear, the officious muse
May safely sing, and sing without reserve.

Vain were the plaint, and ignorant the tear
That should a Talbot mourn. Ourselves, indeed,
Our sinking country, humankind enslaved,
We may lament. But let us, grateful, joy
That ere such virtues gave our days to shine,
Above the dark abyss of modern time,
That we such virtues knew, such virtues felt,
And feel them still, teaching our views to rise
Through ever-brightening scenes of future worlds.
Be dumb, ye worst of zealots! ye that, prone
To thoughtless dust, renounce that generous hope,
Whence every joy below its spirit draws,
And every pain its balm: a Talbot's light,
A Talbot's virtues claim another source
Than the blind maze of undesigning blood;
Nor, when that vital fountain plays no more,
Can they be quenched amid the gelid stream.

Methinks I see his mounting spirit, freed
From tangling earth, regain the realms of day,
Its native country; whence to bless mankind
Eternal goodness on this darksome spot
Had rayed it down a while. Behold! approved
By the tremendous Judge of heaven and earth,
And to the Almighty Father's presence joined,
Whose smile creative beams superior life,
He takes his rank in glory and in bliss
Amid the human worthies. Glad around
Crowd his compatriot shades, and point him out
With noble pride Britannia's blameless boast.
Ah! who is he that with a fonder eye
Meets thine enraptured?—'Tis the best of sons!
The best of friends! Too soon is realized
That hope which once forbad thy tears to flow!
Meanwhile the kindred souls of every land
(Howe'er divided in the fretful days
Of prejudice and error), mingled now,
In one selected never-jarring state,
Where God himself their only monarch reigns,
Partake the joy; yet, such the sense that still
Remains of earthly woes, for us below
And for our loss they drop a pitying tear.
But cease, presumptuous muse, nor vainly strive
To quit this cloudy sphere that binds thee down:
'Tis not for mortal hand to trace these scenes—
Scenes, that our gross ideas grovelling cast
Behind, and strike our boldest language dumb.

Forgive, immortal shade! if aught from earth,
From dust low-warbled, to those groves can rise
Where flows unbidden harmony, forgive
This fond superfluous verse. With deep-felt voice,
On every heart impressed, thy deeds themselves
Attest thy praise. Thy praise the widow's sighs
And orphan's tears embalm. The good, the bad,
The sons of justice and the sons of strife,
All that or freedom or that interest prize,
A deep-divided nation's parties all
Conspire to swell thy spotless praise to heaven.
They catch it there; and to seraphic lyre
Celestial voices thy arrival hail.
How vain this tribute then! this lowly lay!
Yet nothing vain which gratitude inspires.
The muse, besides, her duty thus approves
To virtue, to her country, to mankind,

To forming nature, that in glorious charge,
As to her priestess, has it given to hymn
Whatever good and excellent she forms.

EPITAPH ON MISS ELIZABETH STANLEY, IN HOLYROOD CHURCH, SOUTHAMPTON

Here, Stanley, rest! escaped this mortal strife,
Above the joys, beyond the woes of life,
Fierce pangs no more thy lively beauties stain,
And sternly try thee with a year of pain;
No more sweet patience, feigning oft relief,
Lights thy sick eye to cheat a parent's grief:
With tender art to save her anxious groan,
No more thy bosom presses down its own:
Now well-earned peace is thine, and bliss sincere:
Ours be the lenient, not unpleasing tear!
O born to bloom, then sink beneath the storm;
To show us virtue in her fairest form;
To show us artless reason's moral reign,
What boastful science arrogates in vain;
The obedient passions knowing each their part;
Calm light the head, and harmony the heart!
Yes, we must follow soon, will glad obey;
When a few suns have rolled their cares away,
Tired with vain life, will close the willing eye:
'Tis the great birthright of mankind to die.
Blest be the bark that wafts us to the shore
Where death-divided friends shall part no more:
To join thee there, here with thy dust repose,
Is all the hope thy hapless mother knows.

A POEM TO THE MEMORY OF MR. CONGREVE

ADVERTISEMENT

The author of the following poem, not having had the happiness of a personal acquaintance with Mr. Congreve, is sensible that he has drawn his private character very imperfectly. This all his friends will readily discover: and, therefore, if anyone of them had thought fit to do justice to those amiable qualifications, which made him the love and admiration of all that knew him, these verses had never seen the light.

Oft has the muse, with mean attempt, employed
Her heaven-born voice to flatter prosperous guilt
Or trivial greatness—often stooped her song

To soothe ambition in his frantic rage,
The dire destroyer! while a bleeding world
Wept o'er his crimes. Of this pernicious skill
Unknowing, I these voluntary lays
To genuine worth devote—to worth by all
Confessed and mourned—to Congreve now no more.

First of the fairer kind! by heaven adorned
With every nobler praise, whose smile can lift
The muse unknown to fame, indulgent now
Permit her strain, ennobled by a name,
To all the better few, and chief to thee,
Bright Marlborough, ever sacred, ever dear.

Lamented shade! in him the comic muse,
Parent of gay instruction, lost her loved,
Her last remaining hope; and pensive now
Resigns to folly and his mimic rout
Her throne usurped—presage of darker times,
And deeper woes to come! with taste declined
Fallen virtue droops; and o'er the ill-omened age,
Unseen, unfeared, impend the thousand ills
That wait 'on ignorance: no Congreve now
To scourge our crimes, or laugh to scorn our fools,
A new and nameless herd. Nature was his,
Bold, sprightly, various; and superior art,
Curious to choose each better grace, unseen
Of vulgar eyes; with delicacy free,
Though laboured happy, and though strong refined.
Judgement, severely cool, o'erlooked his toil,
And patient finished all; each fair design
With freedom regular, correctly great,
A master's skilful daring. Closely wrought
His meaning fable, with deep art perplexed,
With striking ease unravelled; no thin plot
Seen through at once and scorned; or ill-concealed
By borrowed aids of mimicry and farce.
His characters strong-featured, equal, just,
From finer nature drawn; and all the mind
Through all her mazes traced; each darker vice,
And darling folly, under each disguise,
By either sex assumed, of studied ease,
False friendship, loose severity, vain wit,
Dull briskness, shallow depth, or coward rage.
Of the whole muse possessed, his piercing eye
Discerned each richer vein of genuine mirth,
Humour or wit; where differing, where agreed;
How counterfeited, or by folly's grin

Or affectation's air; and what their force
To please, to move, to shake the ravished scene
With laughter unreproved. To him the soul,
In all her higher workings, too, was known;
What passions' tumult there; whence their prompt spring,
Their sudden flood of rage, and gradual fall;
Infinite motion! source supreme of bliss
Or woe to man; our heaven or hell below!

Such was his public name; nor less allowed
His private worth; by nature made for praise.
A pleasing form; a soul sincere and clear,
Where all the human graces mixed their charms,
Pure candour, easy goodness, open truth,
Spontaneous all: where strength and beauty joined,
With wit indulgent; humble in the height
Of envied honours; and, but rarely found,
The unjealous friend of every rival worth.
Adorned for social life, each talent his
To win each heart; the charm of happy ease,
Free mirth, gay earning, ever smiling wit,
To all endeared, a pleasure without pain;
What Halifax approved, and Marlborough mourns.

Not so the illiberal mind, where knowledge dwells
Uncouth and harsh, with her attendant, pride,
Impatient of attention, prone to blame,
Disdaining to be pleased; condemning all,
By all condemned; for social joys unfit,
In solitude self-cursed, the child of spleen.
Obliged, ungrateful; unobliged, a foe,
Poor, vicious, old; such fierce-eyed Asper was.
Now meaner Cenus, trivial with design,
Courts poor applause by levity of face,
And scorn of serious thought; to mischief prompt,
Though impotent to wound; profuse of wealth
Yet friendless and unloved; vain, fluttering, false,
A vacant head, and an ungenerous heart.

But slighting these ignoble names, the muse
Pursues her favourite son, and sees him now,
From this dim spot enlarged, triumphant soar
Beyond the walk of time to better worlds,
Where all is new, all wondrous, and all blest!
What art thou, death! by mankind poorly feared,
Yet period of their ills. On thy near shore,
Trembling they stand, and see through dreaded mists
The eternal port, irresolute to leave

This various misery, these air-fed dreams
Which men call life and fame. Mistaken minds!
'Tis reason's prime aspiring, greatly just;
'Tis' happiness supreme, to venture forth
In quest of nobler worlds; to try the deeps
Of dark futurity, with Heaven our guide,
The unerring hand that led us safe through time;
That planted in the soul this powerful hope,
This infinite ambition of new life
And endless joys, still rising, ever new.

These Congreve tastes, safe on the ethereal coast,
Joined to the numberless immortal quire
Of spirits blest. High-seated among these,
He sees the public fathers of mankind,
The greatly good, those universal minds
Who drew the sword, or planned the holy scheme,
For liberty and right, to check the rage
Of blood-stained tyranny and save a world.
Such, high-born Marlborough, be thy sire divine
With wonder named; fair freedom's champion he,
By Heaven approved, a conqueror without guilt,
And such, on earth his friend, and joined on high
By deathless love, Godolphin's patriot worth,
Just to his country's fame, yet of her wealth
With honour frugal; above interest great.
Hail men immortal! social virtues hail!
First heirs of praise!—But I, with weak essay,
Wrong the superior theme; while heavenly quires,
In strains high-warbled to celestial-harps,
Resound your names; and Congreve's added voice
In Heaven exalts what he admired below.

With these he mixes, now no more to swerve
From reason's purest law; no more to please,
Borne by the torrent down, a sensual age.
Pardon, loved shade, that I with friendly blame
Slight note thy error; not to wrong thy worth
Or shade thy memory (far from my soul
Be that base aim I), but haply to deter
From flattering the gross vulgar future pens
Powerful like thine in every grace, and skilled
To win the listening soul with virtuous charms.

If manly thought and wit refined may hope
To please an age in aimless folly sunk,
And sliding swift into the depth of vice!
Consuming pleasure leads the gay and young

Through their vain round, and venal faith the old,
Or avarice mean of soul; instructive arts
Pursued no more; the general taste extinct,
Or all debased; even sacred liberty
The great man's jest, and Britain's welfare named,
By her degenerate sons, the poet's dream,
Or fancy's air-built vision, gaily vain.
Such the lost age; yet still the muse can find,
Superior and apart, a sacred band,
Heroic virtues, who ne'er bowed the knee
To sordid interest; who dare greatly claim
The privilege of men, unfearing truth,
And freedom, heaven's first gift; the ennobling bliss
That renders life of price, and cheaply saved
At life's expense; our sum of happiness.
On these the drooping muses fix their eyes;
From these expect their ancient fame restored.
Nor will the hope be vain; the public weal
With theirs fast linked; a generous truth concealed
From narrow-thoughted power, and known alone
To souls of highest rank. With these, the fair
Be joined in just applause; the brighter few,
Who, raised above gay folly, and the whirl
Of fond amusements, emulate thy praise,
Illustrious Marlborough! pleased, like thee, to shine
Propitious on the muse; whose charms inspire
Her noblest raptures, and whose goodness crowns.

EPISTLES

TO DODINGTON

THE HAPPY MAN

It was to Dodington Thomson dedicated Summer

He's not the happy man to whom is given
A plenteous fortune by indulgent Heaven;
Whose gilded roofs on shining columns rise,
And painted walls enchant the gazer's eyes;
Whose table flows with hospitable cheer,
And all the various bounty of the year;
Whose valleys smile, whose gardens breathe the Spring,
Whose curved mountains bleat, and forests sing;
For whom the cooling shade in Summer twines,
While his full cellars give their generous wines;

From whose wide fields unbounded Autumn pours
A golden tide into his swelling stores:
Whose Winter laughs; for whom the liberal gales
Stretch the big sheet, and toiling commerce sails;
Whom yielding crowds attend, and pleasure serves,
While youth, and health, and vigour string his nerves;
Even not all these, in one rich lot combined,
Can make the happy man, without the mind;
Where judgement sits clear-sighted, and surveys
The chain of reason with unerring gaze;
Where fancy lives, and to the brightening eyes
Bids fairer scenes and bolder figures rise;
Where social love exerts her soft command
And lays the passions with a tender hand,
Whence every virtue flows, in rival strife,
And all the moral harmony of life.
Nor canst thou, Dodington, this truth decline,
Thine is the fortune, and the mind is thine.

TO HIS ROYAL HIGHNESS THE PRINCE OF WALES

On the birth of the Princess Augusta, July 31, 1737

While secret-leaguing nations frown around,
Ready to pour the long-expected storm—
While she who wont the restless Gaul to bound,
Britannia, drooping, grows an empty form—
While on our vitals selfish parties prey
And deep corruption eats our soul away—
Yet in the goddess of the main appears
A gleam of joy, gay-flushing every grace,
As she the cordial voice of millions hears,
Rejoicing zealous o'er thy rising race.
Straight her rekindling eyes resume their fire,
The virtues smile, the muses tune the lyre.
But more enchanting than the muse's song,
United Britons thy dear offspring hail:
The city triumphs through her glowing throng,
The shepherd tells his transport to the dale;
The sons of roughest toil forget their pain,
And the glad sailor cheers the midnight main.
Can aught from fair Augusta's gentle blood,
And thine, thou friend of liberty! be born—
Can aught save what is lovely, generous, good—
What will at once defend us and adorn?
From thence prophetic joy new Edwards eyes;

New Henries, Annas, and Elizas rise.
May fate my fond devoted days extend
To sing the promised glories of thy reign!
What though, by years depressed, my muse might bend?
My heart will teach her still a nobler strain:
How with recovered Britain will she soar,
When France insults, and Spain shall rob no more.

TO THE REV. PATRICK MURDOCH

Thus safely low, my friend, thou canst not fall:
Here reigns a deep tranquillity o'er all;
No noise, no care, no vanity, no strife;
Men, woods, and fields, all breathe untroubled life.
Then keep each passion down, however dear;
Trust me, the tender are the most severe.
Guard, while 'tis thine, thy philosophic ease,
And ask no joy but that of virtuous peace;
That bids defiance to the storms of fate:
High bliss is only for a higher state!

LINES SENT TO GEORGE LYTTELTON, ESQ. SOON AFTER THE DEATH OF HIS WIFE: WRITTEN IN A COPY OF 'THE SEASONS '

Go, little book, and find our friend,
Who nature and the muses loves,
Whose cares the public virtues blend
With all the softness of the groves.
A fitter time thou canst not choose
His fostering friendship to repay;
Go then, and try, my rural muse,
To steal his widowed hours away.

TO MRS. MENDEZ' BIRTHDAY

Who was born on Valentine's Day.

Thine is the gentle day of love
When youths and virgins try their fate;
When, deep retiring to the grove,
Each feathered songster weds his mate.
With tempered beams the skies are bright,

Earth decks in smiles her pleasing face;
Such is the day that gave thee light,
And speaks as such thy every grace.

TO THE INCOMPARABLE SOPORIFIC DOCTOR

*The Rev. Dr. Patrick Murdoch, Thomson's old and intimate friend and countryman—afterwards his kindly
biographer. He was presented to the living of Stradishall in Suffolk in 1737-8 by Admiral Vernon, of Great
Thurlow, to whose son he had been tutor. In 1760 he became vicar of Great Thurlow, where he wrote his
memoir of the poet*

Sweet, sleeky Doctor! dear pacific soul!
Lay at the beef, and suck the vital bowl!
Still let the involving smoke around thee fly,
And broad-looked dullness settle in thine eye.
Ah! soft in down those dainty limbs repose,
And in the very lap of slumber doze;
But chiefly on the lazy day of grace,
Call forth the lambent glories of thy face;
If aught the thoughts of dinner can prevail—
And sure the Sunday's dinner cannot fail.
To the thin church in sleepy pomp proceed,
And lean on the lethargic book thy head.
Those eyes wipe often with the hallowed lawn,
Profoundly nod, immeasurably yawn.
Slow let the prayers by thy meek lips be sung.
Nor let thy thoughts be distanced by thy tongue
If e'er the lingerers are within a call,
Or if on prayers thou deign'st to think at all.
Yet—only yet—the swimming head we bend;
But when serene, the pulpit you ascend,
Through every joint a gentle horror creeps,
And round you the consenting audience sleeps.
So when an ass with sluggish front appears,
The horses start, and prick their quivering ears;
But soon as e'er the sage is heard to bray,
The fields all thunder, and they bound away.

TO SERAPHINA

The wanton's charms, however bright,
Are like the false illusive light
Whose flattering unauspicious blaze
To precipices oft betrays.

But that sweet ray your beauties dart,
Which clears the mind and cleans the heart,
Is like the sacred queen of night
Who pours a lovely gentle light
Wide o'er the dark—by wanderers blest,
Conducting them to peace and rest.

A vicious love depraves the mind;
'Tis anguish, guilt, and folly joined;
But Seraphina's eyes dispense
A mild and gracious influence,
Such as in visions angels shed
Around the heaven-illumined head.

To love thee, Seraphina, sure
Is to be tender, happy, pure;
'Tis from low passions to escape,
And woo bright virtue's fairest shape;
'Tis ecstasy with wisdom joined,
And heaven infused into the mind.

TO AMANDA

IN IMITATION OF TIBULLUS

Hue ades, et tenerae morbos expelle puellae,
Hue ades, intonsa Phoebe superbe coma, &c.
Tibulli Lib. IV, Gar. iv.

Come, healing god! Apollo, come and aid,
Moved by the tears of love, my tender maid!
No more let sickness dim those radiant eyes
Which never know to cheat or to disguise.
If e'er my verse has pleased thy listening ear,
O now be friendly, now propitious hear!
Bring every virtuous herb, each root and flower
Of cooling juice and salutary power.
Light is the task: to touch a hand so fair,
Divine physician, will repay thy care.

My tears are fled; the god my suit approves;
He can't be wretched who sincerely loves.
Protecting Heaven, with more than common care,
Smiles on his hopes and guards him from despair.

Raise from the pillow, raise thy languid head;
Come forth, my love, and quit thy sickly bed!
Come forth, my love! for thee the balmy Spring
Breathes every sweet; for thee the zephyrs bring
Their healing gales; for thee the graces lead
The smiling hours, and paint the flowery mead.
As nature, drooping long beneath the reign
Of dreary winter, now revives again,
Calls all her beauties out, and charms us more
From what we suffered in their loss before;
So from thy tedious illness shalt thou rise
More sweetly fair; and in those languid eyes
And faded cheeks returning health shall place
A fresher bloom and more attractive grace.
Then shall my bounding heart forget its woe,
And think it never more a pain can know;
Then shall my muse thy charms more gaily sing,
And hail thee as the nightingale the spring.

TO AMANDA

Ah! urged too late, from beauty's bondage free,
Why did I trust my liberty with thee?
And thou, why didst thou with inhuman art,
If not resolved to take, seduce my heart?
Yes, yes! you said—for lovers' eyes speak true;
You must have seen how fast my passion grew:
And, when your glances chanced on me to shine,
How my fond soul ecstatic sprung to thine!

But mark me, fair one! what I now declare
Thy deep attention claims and serious care:
It is no common passion fires my breast—
I must be wretched, or I must be blest!
My woes all other remedy deny—
Or pitying give me hope, or bid me die!

TO AMANDA, WITH A COPY OF 'THE SEASONS'

Accept, loved Nymph, this tribute due
To tender friendship, love, and you;
But with it take what breathed the whole,
O take to thine the poet's soul
If fancy here her power displays,

And if a heart exalts these lays,
You fairest in that fancy shine,
And all that heart is fondly thine.

MISCELLANEOUS POEMS

BRITANNIA: A POEM

Written in 1727, published in January, 1729

—Et tantas audetis tollere moles?
Quos ego-sed motos praestat componere fluctus.
Post mihi non simili poena commissa luetis.
Maturate fugam, regique haec dicite vestro:
Non illi imperium pelagi, saevumque tridentem,
Sed mihi sorte datum. VIRGIL,. Aeneid, i. 134.

As on the sea-beat shore Britannia sat,
Of her degenerate sons the faded fame
Deep in her anxious heart revolving sad—
Bare was her throbbing bosom to the gale,
That, hoarse and hollow, from the bleak surge blew;
Loose flowed her tresses; rent her azure robe.
Hung o'er the deep from her majestic brow
She tore the laurel, and she tore the bay.
Nor ceased the copious grief to bathe her cheek;
Nor ceased her sobs to murmur to the main.
Peace discontented, nigh departing, stretched
Her dove-like wings; and War, though greatly roused,
Yet mourns his fettered hands; while thus the queen
Of nations spoke; and what she said the muse
Recorded faithful in unbidden verse:—

'Even not yon sail, that from the sky-mixed wave
Dawns on the sight, and wafts the royal youth,
A freight of future glory, to my shore;
Even not the flattering view of golden days,
And rising periods yet of bright renown,
Beneath the Parents, and their endless line
Through late revolving time, can soothe my rage;
While, unchastised, the insulting Spaniard dares
Infest the trading flood, full of vain war
Despise my navies, and my merchants seize;
As, trusting to false peace, they fearless roam
The world of waters wild; made, by the toil,
And liberal blood of glorious ages, mine:

Nor bursts my sleeping thunder on their head.
Whence this unwonted patience? this weak doubt?
This tame beseeching of rejected peace?
This meek forbearance? this unnative fear,
To generous Britons never known before?
And sailed my fleets for this—on Indian tides
To float, inactive, with the veering winds?
The mockery of war! while hot disease
And sloth distempered swept off burning crowds,
For action ardent; and amid the deep,
Inglorious, sunk them in a watery grave.
There now they lie beneath the rolling flood,
Far from their friends, and country, unavenged;
And back the drooping warship comes again,
Dispirited and thin; her sons ashamed
Thus idly to review their native shore;
With not one glory sparkling in their eye,
One triumph on their tongue. A passenger,
The violated merchant comes along—
That far sought wealth, for which the noxious gale
He drew, and sweat beneath equator suns—
By lawless force detained, a force that soon
Would melt away, and every spoil resign,
Were once the British lion heard to roar.
Whence is it that the proud Iberian thus
In their own well asserted element
Dares rouse to wrath the masters of the main?
Who told him that the big incumbent war
Would not, ere this, have rolled his trembling ports
In smoky ruin? and his guilty stores,
Won by the ravage of a butchered world,
Yet unatoned, sunk in the swallowing deep,
Or led the glittering prize into the Thames?

'There was a time (oh, let my languid sons
Resume their spirit at the rousing thought!)
When all the pride of Spain, in one dread fleet,
Swelled o'er the labouring surge like a whole heaven
Of clouds wide-rolled before the boundless breeze.
Gaily the splendid armament along
Exultant ploughed, reflecting a red gleam,
As sunk the sun, o'er all the flaming vast;
Tall, gorgeous, and elate; drunk with the dream
Of easy conquest; while their bloated war,
Stretched out from sky to sky, the gathered force
Of ages held in its capacious womb.
But soon, regardless of the cumbrous pomp,
My dauntless Britons came, a gloomy few,

With tempests black, the goodly scene deformed,
And laid their glory waste. The bolts of fate
Resistless thundered through their yielding sides;
Fierce o'er their beauty blazed the lurid flame;
And seized in horrid grasp, or shattered wide
Amid the mighty waters, deep they sunk.
Then too from every promontory chill,
Rank fen, and cavern where the wild wave works,
I swept confederate-winds, and swelled a storm.
Round the glad isle, snatched by the vengeful blast,
The scattered remnants drove; on the blind shelve,
And pointed rock that marks the indented shore,
Relentless dashed, where—loud the northern main—
Howls through the, fractured Caledonian isles.

'Such were the dawnings of my liquid reign;
But since, how vast it grew, how absolute,
Even in those troubled times when dreadful Blake
Awed angry nations with the British name,
Let every humbled state, let Europe say,
Sustained and balanced by my naval arm.
Ah, what must those immortal spirits think
Of your poor shifts? Those, for their country's good,
Who faced the blackest danger, knew no fear,
No mean submission, but commanded peace—
Ah, how with indignation must they burn!
(If aught but joy can touch ethereal breasts)
With shame! with grief! to see their feeble sons
Shrink from that empire o'er the conquered seas
For which their wisdom planned, their councils glowed,
And their veins bled through many a toiling age.

'Oh, first of human blessings, and supreme!
Fair Peace! how lovely, how delightful thou!
By whose wide tie the kindred sons of men
Like brothers live, in amity combined
And unsuspicious faith; while honest toil
Gives every joy, and to those joys a right,
Which idle, barbarous rapine but usurps.
Pure is thy reign; when, unaccursed by blood,
Nought, save the sweetness of indulgent showers,
Trickling distils into the vernant glebe;
Instead of mangled carcasses, sad—seen,
When the blithe sheaves lie scattered o'er the field;
When only shining shares, the crooked knife,
And hooks imprint the vegetable wound;
When the land blushes with the rose alone,
The falling fruitage and the bleeding vine.

Oh, Peace! thou source and soul of social life,
Beneath whose calm inspiring influence,
Science his views enlarges, Art refines,
And swelling Commerce opens all her ports,
Blest be the man divine who gives us thee!
Who bids the trumpet hush his horrid clang,
Nor blow the giddy nations into rage;
Who sheathes the murderous blade; the deadly gun
Into the well piled armoury returns;
And every vigour from the work of death
To grateful industry converting, makes
The country flourish, and the city smile.
Unviolated, him the virgin sings;
And him the smiling mother to her train.
Of him the shepherd in the peaceful dale
Chants; and, the treasures of his labour sure,
The husbandman of him, as at the plough
Or team he toils. With him the sailor soothes,
Beneath the trembling moon, the midnight wave;
And the full city, warm from street to street,
And shop to shop responsive, rings of him.
Nor joys one land alone: his praise extends
Far as the sun rolls the diffusive day,
Far as the breeze can bear the gifts of peace,
Till all the happy nations catch the song.

'What would not, Peace! the patriot bear for thee?
What painful patience? what incessant care?
What mixed anxiety? what sleepless toil?
Even from the rash protected what reproach?
For he thy value knows; thy friendship he
To human nature: but the better thou,
The richer of delight, sometimes the more
Inevitable war; when ruffian force
Awakes the fury of an injured state.
Then the good easy man, whom reason rules,
Who, while unhurt, knew nor offence nor harm,
Roused by bold insult, and injurious rage,
With sharp and sudden check the astonished sons
Of violence confounds; firm as his cause,
His bolder heart; in awful justice clad;
His eyes effulging a peculiar fire:
And, as he charges through the prostrate war,
His keen arm teaches faithless men, no more
To dare the sacred vengeance of the just.

'And what, my thoughtless sons, should fire you more
Than when your well-earned empire of the deep

The least beginning injury receives?
What better cause can call your lightning forth?
Your thunder wake? your dearest life demand?
What better cause, than when your country sees
The sly destruction at her vitals aimed?
For oh! it much imports you, 'tis your all,
To keep your trade entire, entire the force
And honour of your fleets—o'er that to watch,
Even with a hand severe and jealous eye.
In intercourse be gentle, generous, just,
By wisdom polished, and of manners fair;
But on the sea be terrible, untamed,
Unconquerable—still: let none escape
Who shall but aim to touch your glory there.
Is there the man into the lion's den
Who dares intrude, to snatch his young away?
And is a Briton seized? and seized beneath
The slumbering terrors of a British fleet?
Then ardent rise! Oh, great in vengeance, rise!
O'erturn the proud, teach rapine to restore:
And, as you ride sublimely round the world,
Make every vessel stoop, make every state
At once their welfare and their duty know.
This is your glory, this your wisdom; this
The native power for which you were designed
By fate, when fate designed the firmest state
That e'er was seated on the subject sea;
A state, alone, where Liberty should live,
In these late times, this evening of mankind,
When Athens, Rome, and Carthage are no more,
The world almost in slavish sloth dissolved.
For this, these rocks around your coast were thrown;
For this, your oaks, peculiar hardened, shoot
Strong into sturdy growth: for this, your hearts
Swell with a sullen courage, growing still
As danger grows; and strength, and toil for this
Are liberal poured o'er all the fervent land.
Then cherish this, this unexpensive power,
Undangerous to the public, ever prompt,
By lavish nature thrust into your hand:
And, unencumbered with the bulk immense
Of conquest, whence huge empires rose, and fell
Self-crushed, extend your reign from shore to shore,
Where'er the wind your high behests can blow;
And fix it deep on this eternal base.
For, should the sliding fabric once give way,
Soon slackened quite, and past recovery broke,
It gathers ruin as it rolls along,

Steep rushing down to that devouring gulf
Where many a mighty empire buried lies.
And should the big redundant flood of trade,
In which ten thousand thousand labours join
Their several currents, till the boundless tide
Rolls in a radiant deluge o'er the land;
Should this bright stream, the least inflected, point
Its course another way, o'er other lands
The various treasure would resistless pour,
Ne'er to be won again; its ancient tract
Left a vile channel, desolate, and dead,
With all around a miserable waste.
Not Egypt, were her better heaven, the Nile,
Turned in the pride of flow; when o'er his rocks,
And roaring cataracts, beyond the reach
Of dizzy vision piled, in one wide flash
An Ethiopian deluge foams amain
(Whence wondering fable traced him from the sky);
Even not that prime of earth, where harvests crowd
On untilled harvests, all the teeming year,
If of the fat o'erflowing culture robbed,
Were then a more uncomfortable wild,
Sterile, and void; than of her trade deprived,
Britons, your boasted-isle: her princes sunk;
Her high built honour mouldered to the dust;
Unnerved her force; her spirit vanished quite;
With rapid wing her riches fled away;
Her unfrequented ports alone the sign
Of what she was; her merchants scattered wide;
Her hollow shops shut up; and in her streets,
Her fields, woods, markets, villages, and roads
The cheerful voice of labour heard no more.

'Oh, let not then waste luxury impair
That manly soul of toil which strings your nerves,
And your own proper happiness creates!
Oh, let not the soft penetrating plague
Creep on the freeborn mind! and working there,
With the sharp tooth of many a new-formed want,
Endless, and idle all, eat out the heart
Of liberty; the high conception blast;
The noble sentiment, the impatient scorn
Of base subjection, and the swelling wish
For general good, erasing from the mind:
While nought save narrow selfishness succeeds,
And low design, the sneaking passions all
Let loose, and reigning in the rankled breast.
Induced at last, by scarce perceived degrees,

Sapping the very frame of government
And life, a total dissolution comes;
Sloth, ignorance, dejection, flattery, fear,
Oppression raging o'er the waste he makes;
The human being almost quite extinct;
And the whole state in broad corruption sinks.
Oh, shun that gulf: that gaping ruin shun!
And countless ages roll it far away
From you, ye heaven-beloved! May liberty,
The light of life! the sun of humankind!
Whence heroes, bards, and patriots borrow flame,
Even where the keen depressive north descends,
Still spread, exalt, and actuate your powers!
While slavish southern climates beam in vain.
And may a public spirit from the throne,
Where every virtue sits, go copious forth,
Live o'er the land! the finer arts inspire;
Make thoughtful Science raise his pensive head,
Blow the fresh bay, bid Industry rejoice,
And the rough sons of lowest labour smile:
As when, profuse of Spring, the loosened west
Lifts up the pining year, and balmy breathes
Youth, life, and love, and beauty o'er the world.

'But haste we from these melancholy shores,
Nor to deaf winds, and waves, our fruitless plaint
Pour weak; the country claims our active aid;
That let us roam; and where we find a spark,
Of public virtue, blow it into flame.
Lo! now, my sons, the sons of freedom! meet
In awful senate; thither let us fly;
Burn in the patriot's thought, flow from his tongue
In fearless truth; myself transformed preside,
And shed the spirit of Britannia round.'

This said, her fleeting form and airy train
Sunk in the gale; and nought but ragged rocks
Rushed on the broken eye, and nought was heard
But the rough cadence of the dashing wave.

A PARAPHRASE OF THE LATTER PART OF THE SIXTH CHAPTER OF ST. MATTHEW

When my breast labours with oppressive care,
And o'er my cheek descends the falling tear;
While all my warring passions are at strife,
Oh, let me listen to the words of Life!

Raptures deep-felt his doctrine did impart,
And thus he raised from earth the drooping heart:—

'Think not, when all your scanty stores afford
Is spread at once upon the sparing board—
Think not, when worn the homely robe appears,
While on the roof the howling tempest bears—
What farther shall this feeble life sustain,
And what shall clothe these shivering limbs again.
Say, does not life its nourishment exceed?
And the fair body its investing weed?
Behold! and look away your low despair—
See the light tenants of the barren air:
To them nor stores nor granaries belong,
Nought but the woodland and the pleasing song;
Yet your kind heavenly Father bends his eye
On the least wing that flits along the sky.
To him they sing when Spring renews the plain,
To him they cry in Winter's pinching reign;
Nor is, their music, nor their plaint in vain
He hears the gay and the distressful call,
And with unsparing bounty fills them all.
Observe the rising lily's snowy grace;
Observe the various vegetable race;
They neither toil nor spin, but careless grow;
Yet see how warm they blush! how bright they glow!
What regal vestments can with them compare?
What king so shining, and what queen so fair?
If ceaseless thus the fowls of heaven he feeds,
If o'er the fields such lucid robes he spreads;
Will he not care for you, ye faithless, say?
Is he unwise? or are ye less than they?'

ON THE REPORT OF A WOODEN BRIDGE TO BE BUILT AT WESTMINSTER

By Rufus' hall, where Thames polluted flows,
Provoked, the Genius of the river rose,
And thus exclaimed: 'Have I, ye British swains,
Have I for ages laved your fertile plains?
Given herds, and flocks, and villages increase,
And fed a richer than the golden fleece?
Have I, ye merchants, with each swelling tide,
Poured Afrie's treasure in, and India's pride?
Lent you the fruit of every nation's toil?
Made every climate yours, and every soil?
Yet, pilfered from the poor, by gaming base,

Yet must a wooden bridge my waves disgrace?
Tell not to foreign streams the shameful tale,
And be it published in no Gallic vale.'
He said; and, plunging to his crystal dome,
White o'er his head the circling waters foam.

JUVENILIA

THE WORKS AND WONDERS OF ALMIGHTY POWER

A FRAGMENT

Now I surveyed my native faculties,
And traced my actions to their teeming source.
Now I explored the universal frame;
Gazed nature through, and with interior light
Conversed with angels and unbodied saints,
That tread the courts of the Eternal King!
Gladly would I declare, in lofty strains,
The power of Godhead to the sons of men.
But thought is lost in its immensity;
Imagination wastes its strength in vain;
And fancy tires, and turns within itself,
Struck with the amazing depths of Deity!

Ah! my loved God! in vain a tender youth
Unskilled in arts of deep philosophy,
Attempts to search the bulky mass of matter;
To trace the rules of motion; and pursue
The phantom Time, too subtile for his grasp!
Yet may I, from thy most apparent works,
Form some idea of their wondrous Author,
And celebrate thy praise with rapturous mind!

How can I gaze upon yon sparkling vault,
And view the planets rolling in their spheres,
Yet be an atheist? Can I see those stars,
And think of others far beyond my ken,
Yet want conviction of creating power?
What but a Being of immense perfection
Could, through unbounded spaces, thus dispose
Such numerous bodies, all presumptive worlds?
The undesigning hand of giddy chance
Could never fill, with globes so vast, so bright,
That lofty concave!
Where shall I trace the sources of the light?

What seats assign the element of fire,
That, unconfined, through all the systems breaks?
Here could I lie, in holy contemplation rapt,
And pass with pleasure an eternal age!
But 'tis too much for my weak mind to know.
Teach me with humble reverence to adore
The mysteries I must not comprehend!

A PARAPHRASE OF PSALM CIV

To praise thy Author, Soul, do not forget;
Canst thou, in gratitude, deny the debt?
Lord, thou art great, how great we cannot know;
Honour and majesty do round thee flow.
The purest rays of primogenial light
Compose thy robes, and make them dazzling bright;
The heavens and all the wide-spread orbs on high
Thou like a curtain stretched of curious dye;
On the devouring flood thy chambers are
Established; a lofty cloud's thy car,
Which quick through the ethereal road doth fly
On swift-winged winds that shake the troubled sky.
Of spiritual substance angels thou didst frame,
Active and bright, piercing and quick as flame.
Thou hast firmly founded this unwieldy earth;
Stand fast for aye, thou saidst, at nature's birth.
The swelling flood thou o'er the earth mad'st creep,
And coveredst it with the vast hoary deep:
Then hills and vales did no distinction know,
But levelled nature lay oppressed below.
With speed they, at thy awful thunder's roar,
Shrinked within the limits of their shore.
Through secret tracts they up the mountains creep,
And rocky caverns fruitful moisture weep,
Which sweetly through the verdant vales doth glide,
Till 'tis devoured by the greedy tide.
The feeble sands thou hast made the ocean's mounds;
Its foaming waves shall ne'er repass these bounds,
Again to triumph over the dry grounds.
Between the hills, grazed by the bleating kind,
Soft warbling rills their mazy way do find—
By him appointed fully to supply,
When the hot dogstar fires the realms on high,
The raging thirst of every sickening beast,
Of the wild ass that roams the dreary waste.
The feathered nation, by their smiling sides,

In lowly brambles or in trees abides;
By nature taught, on them they rear their nests,
That with inimitable art are dressed.
They for the shade and safety of the wood
With natural music cheer the neighbourhood.
He doth the clouds with genial moisture fill,
Which on the ground they bounteously distil,
And nature's lap with various blessings crowd:
The giver, God! all creatures cry aloud.
With freshest green he clothes the fragrant mead,
Whereon the grazing herds wanton and feed.
With vital juice he makes the plants abound,
And herbs securely spring above the ground,
That man may be sustained beneath the toil
Of manuring the ill-producing soil,—
Which with a plenteous harvest does at last
Cancel the memory of labours past,
Yields him the product of the generous vine,
And balmy oil that makes his face to shine,
Fills all his granaries with a loaden crop,
Against the barren winter his great prop.
The trees of God with kindly sap do swell,
Even cedars tall in Lebanon that dwell,
Upon whose lofty tops the birds erect
Their nests, as careful nature does direct.
The long necked storks unto the fir-trees fly,
And with their crackling cries disturb the sky.
To unfrequented hills wild goats resort,
And on bleak rocks the nimble conies sport.
The changing moon he clad with silver light,
To check the black dominion of the night:
High through the skies in silent state she rides,
And by her rounds the fleeting time divides.
The circling sun doth in due time decline,
And unto shades the murmuring world resign.
Dark night thou mak'st succeed the cheerful day,
Which forest beasts from their lone caves survey:
They rouse themselves, creep out, and search their prey.
Young hungry lions from their dens come out,
And, mad on blood, stalk fearfully about;
They break night's silence with their hideous roar,
And from kind heaven their nightly prey implore.
Just as the lark begins to stretch her wing,
And, flickering on her nest, makes short essays to sing,
And the sweet dawn, with a faint glimmering light,
Unveils the face of nature to the sight,
To their dark dens they take their hasty flight.
Not so the husbandman,—for with the sun

He does his pleasant course of labours run:
Home with content in the cool e'en returns,
And his sweet toils until the morn adjourns.
How many are thy wondrous works, O Lord!
They of thy wisdom solid proofs afford:
Out of thy boundless goodness thou didst fill,
With riches and delights, both vale and hill:
Even the broad ocean, wherein do abide
Monsters that flounce upon the boiling tide,
And swarms of lesser beasts and fish beside.
'Tis there that daring ships before the wind
Do scud amain, and make the port assigned:
'Tis there that Leviathan sports and plays,
And spouts his water in the face of day;
For food with gaping mouth they wait on thee,
If thou withhold'st, they pine, they faint, they die.
Thou bountifully opest thy liberal hand,
And scatterest plenty both on sea and land.
Thy vital Spirit makes all things live below,
The face of nature with new beauties glow.
God's awful glory ne'er will have an end,
To vast eternity it will extend.
When he surveys his works, at the wide sight
He doth rejoice, and take divine delight.
His looks the earth into its centre shakes;
A touch of his to smoke the mountains makes.
I'll to God's honour consecrate my lays,
And when I cease to be I'll cease to praise.
Upon the Lord, a sublime lofty theme,
My meditations sweet, my joys supreme.
Let daring sinners feel thy vengeful rod,
May they no more be known by their abode.
My soul and all my powers, O bless the Lord,
And the whole race of men with one accord.

A COMPLAINT ON THE MISERIES OF LIFE

I loathe, O Lord, this life below,
And all its fading fleeting joys;
'Tis a short space that's filled with woe,
Which all our bliss by far outweighs.
When will the everlasting morn
With dawning light the skies adorn?

Fitly this life's compared to night,
When gloomy darkness shades the sky;

Just like the morn's our glimmering light
Reflected from the Deity.
When will celestial morn dispel
These dark surrounding shades of hell?

I'm sick of this vexatious state,
Where cares invade my peaceful hours;
Strike the last blow, O courteous fate,
I'll smiling fall like mowed flowers;
I'll gladly spurn this clogging clay,
And, sweetly singing, soar away.

What's money but refined dust?
What's honour but an empty name?
And what is soft enticing lust
But a consuming idle flame?
Yea, what is all beneath the sky
But emptiness and vanity?

With thousand ills our life's oppressed;
There's nothing here worth living for!
In the lone grave I long to rest,
And be harassed here no more:
Where joy's fantastic; grief's sincere,
And. where there's nought for which I care.

Thy word, O Lord, shall be my guide;
Heaven, where thou dwellest is my goal;
Through corrupt life grant I may glide
With an untainted upward soul.
Then may this life, this dreary night
Dispelled be by morning light.

HYMN ON THE POWER OF GOD

Hail! Power Divine, whose sole command
From the dark empty space
Made the broad sea and solid land
Smile with a heavenly grace;

Made the high mountain and firm rock,
Where bleating cattle stray;
And the strong, stately, spreading oak,
That intercepts the day.

The rolling planets thou mad'st move,

By thy effective will;
And the revolving globes above
Their destined course fulfil.

His mighty power, ye thunders, praise,
As through the heavens you roll;
And his great name, ye lightnings, blaze
Unto the distant pole.

Ye seas, in your eternal roar
His sacred praise proclaim;
While the inactive sluggish shore
Re-echoes to the same.

Ye howling winds, howl out his praise,
And make the forests bow;
While through the air, the earth, and seas
His solemn praise ye blow.

O you, ye high harmonious spheres,
Your powerful mover sing;
To him, your circling course that steers,
Your tuneful praises bring.

Ungrateful mortals, catch the sound,
And in your numerous lays
To all the listening world around
The God of nature praise.

A PASTORAL BETWIXT DAVID, THIRSIS, AND THE ANGEL GABRIEL, UPON THE BIRTH OF OUR SAVIOUR

DAVID:
What means yon apparition in the sky,
Thirsis, that dazzles every shepherd's eye?
I slumbering was when from yon glorious cloud
Came gliding music heavenly, sweet, and loud,
With sacred raptures which my bosom fires,
And with celestial joy my soul inspires;
It soothes the native horrors of the night,
And gladdens nature more than dawning light.

THIRSIS:
But hold! see hither through the yielding air
An angel comes: for mighty news prepare.

ANGEL GABRIEL:

Rejoice, ye swains, anticipate the morn
With songs of praise; for lo! a Saviour's born.
With joyful haste to Bethlehem repair,
And you will find the almighty Infant there;
Wrapped in a swaddling band you'll find your King,
And in a manger laid: to him your praises bring.

CHORUS OF ANGELS:
To God who in the highest dwells
Immortal glory be;
Let peace be in the humble cells
Of Adam's progeny.

DAVID:
No more the year shall wintry horrors bring;
Fixed in the indulgence of eternal spring,
Immortal green shall clothe the hills and vales,
And odorous sweets shall load the balmy gales;
The silver brooks shall in soft murmurs tell
The joy that shall their oozy channels swell.
Feed on, my flocks, and crop the tender grass;
Let blooming joy appear on every face,
For lo! this blessed, this propitious morn,
The Saviour of lost mankind is born.

THIRSIS:
Thou fairest morn that ever sprang from night,
Or decked the opening skies with rosy light,
Well mayst thou shine with a distinguished ray,
Since here Emmanuel condescends to stay,
Our fears, our guilt, our darkness to dispel,
And save us from the horrid jaws of hell;
Who from his throne descended, matchless love!
To guide poor mortals to blest seats above.
But come! without delay let us be gone;
Shepherd, let's go, and humbly kiss the Son.

PASTORAL BETWEEN THIRSIS AND CORYDON UPON THE DEATH OF DAMON

By Damon is meant Mr. W. Riddell

THIRSIS:
Say, tell me true, what is the doleful cause
That Corydon is not the man he was?
Your cheerful presence used to lighten cares,
And from the plains to banish gloomy fears.

Whene'er unto the circling swains you sung,
Our ravished souls upon the music hung;
The gazing, listening flocks forgot their meat,
While vocal grottoes did your lays repeat:
But now your gravity our mirth rebukes,
And in your downcast and desponding looks
Appears some fatal and impending woe;
I fear to ask, and yet desire to know.

CORYDON:
The doleful news, how shall I, Thirsis, tell!
In blooming youth the hapless Damon fell:
He's dead, he's dead! and with him all my joy;
The mournful thought does all gay forms destroy:
This is the cause of my unusual grief,
Which sullenly admits of no relief.

THIRSIS:
Begone all mirth! begone all sports and play!
To a deluge of grief and tears give way.
Damon the just, the generous, and the young,
Must Damon's worth and merit be unsung?
No, Corydon! the wondrous youth you knew,
How, as in years, so he in virtue grew;
Embalm his fame in never dying verse,
As a just tribute to his doleful hearse.

CORYDON:
Assist me, mighty grief; my breast inspire
With generous heats and with thy wildest fire,
While in a solemn and a mournful strain
Of Damon gone for ever I complain.
Ye muses, weep; your mirth and songs forbear,
And for him sigh and shed a friendly tear;
He was your favourite, and by your aid
In charming verse his witty thoughts arrayed;
He had of knowledge, learning, wit a store;
To it denied he still pressed after more.
He was a pious and a virtuous soul,
And still pressed forward to the heavenly goal;
He was a faithful, true, and constant friend,
Faithful, and true, and constant to the end.
Ye flowers, hang down and droop your [heavy] heads,
No more around your grateful odour spreads;
Ye leafy trees, your blooming honours shed,
Damon for ever from your shade is fled;
Fled to the mansions of eternal light,
Where endless wonders strike his happy sight.

Ye birds, be mute, as through the trees you fly,
Mute as the grave wherein my friend does lie.
Ye winds, breathe sighs as through the air you rove,
And in sad pomp the trembling branches move.
Ye gliding brooks, O weep your channels dry,
My flowing tears them fully shall supply;
You in soft murmurs may your grief express,
And yours, you swains, in mournful songs confess
I to some dark and gloomy shade will fly,
Dark as the grave wherein my friend does lie;
And for his death to lonely rocks complain
In mournful accents and a dying strain,
While pining echo answers me again.

OF A COUNTRY LIFE

I hate the clamours of the smoky towns,
But much admire the bliss of rural clowns;
Where some remains of innocence appear,
Where no rude noise insults the listening ear;
Nought but soft zephyrs whispering through the trees,
Or the still humming of the painful bees;
The gentle murmurs of a purling rill,
Or the unwearied chirping of the drill;
The charming harmony of warbling birds,
Or hollow lowings of the grazing herds;
The murmuring stockdoves' melancholy coo,
When they their loved mates lament or woo;
The pleasing bleatings of the tender lambs,
Or the indistinct mumbling of their dams;
The musical discord of chiding hounds,
Whereto the echoing hill or rock resounds;
The rural mournful songs of lovesick swains,
Whereby they soothe their raging amorous pains;
The whistling music of the lagging plough,
Which does the strength of drooping beasts renew.

And as the country rings with pleasant sounds,
So with delightful prospects it abounds:
Through every season of the sliding year,
Unto the ravished sight new scenes appear.
In the sweet Spring the sun's prolific ray
Does painted flowers to the mild air display;
Then opening buds, then tender herbs are seen,
And the bare fields are all arrayed in green.

In ripening Summer, the full laden vales
Gives prospect of employment for the flails;
Each breath of wind the bearded groves makes bend,
Which seems the fatal sickle to portend.

In Autumn, that repays. the labourer's pains,
Reapers sweep down the honours of the plains.

Anon black Winter, from the frozen north,
Its treasuries of snow and hail pours forth;
Then stormy winds blow through the hazy sky;
In desolation nature seems to lie;
The unstained snow from the full clouds descends,
Whose sparkling lustre open eyes offends.
In maiden white the glittering fields do shine;
Then bleating flocks for want of food repine,
With withered eyes they see all snow around,
And with their fore feet paw, and scrape the ground:
They cheerfully do crop the insipid grass,
The shepherds sighing, cry, Alas! alas!
Then pinching want the wildest beast does tame;
Then huntsmen on the snow do trace their game;
Keen frost then turns the liquid lakes to glass,
Arrests the dancing rivulets as they pass. 50

How sweet and innocent are country sports,
And, as men's tempers, various are their sorts.
You, on the banks of soft meandering Tweed,
May in your toils ensnare the watery breed,
And nicely lead the artificial flee,
Which, when the nimble, watchful trout does see,
He at the bearded hook will briskly spring;
Then in that instant twitch your hairy string,
And, when he's hooked, you, with a constant hand,
May draw him struggling to the fatal land.

Then at fit seasons you may clothe your hook
With a sweet bait, dressed by a faithless cook
The greedy pike darts to't with eager haste,
And, being struck, in vain he flies at last;
He rages, storms, and flounces through the stream,
But all, alas! his life can not redeem.

At other times you may pursue the chase,
And hunt the nimble hare from place to place.
See, when the dog is just upon the grip,
Out at a side she'll make a handsome skip,
And ere he can divert his furious course,

She, far before him, scours with all her force:
She'll shift, and many times run the same ground;
At last, outwearied by the stronger hound,
She falls a sacrifice unto his hate,
And with sad piteous screams laments her fate.

See how the hawk doth take his towering flight,
And in his course outflies our very sight,
Beats down the fluttering fowl with all his might.

See how the wary gunner casts about,
Watching the fittest posture when to shoot:
Quick as the fatal lightning blasts the oak,
He gives the springing fowl a sudden stroke;
He pours upon't a shower of mortal lead,
And ere the noise is heard the fowl is dead.

Sometimes he spreads his hidden subtile snare,
Of which the entangled fowl was not aware;
Through pathless wastes he doth pursue his sport,
Where nought but moor-fowl and wild beasts resort.

When the noon sun directly darts his beams go
Upon your giddy heads, with fiery gleams,
Then you may bathe yourself in cooling streams;
Or to the sweet adjoining grove retire,
Where trees with interwoven boughs conspire
To form a grateful shade; there rural swains
Do tune their oaten reeds to rural strains;
The silent birds sit listening on the sprays,
And in soft charming notes do imitate their lays.
There you may stretch yourself upon the grass,
And, lulled with music, to kind slumbers pass:
No meagre cares your fancy will distract,
And on that scene no tragic fears will act;
Save the dear image of a charming she,
Nought will the object of your vision be.

Away the vicious pleasures of the town!
Let empty partial fortune on me frown;
But grant, ye powers, that it may be my lot
To live in peace from noisy towns remote.

UPON HAPPINESS

Warmed by the summer sun's meridian ray,

As underneath a spreading oak I lay,
Contemplating the mighty load of woe
In search of bliss that mortals undergo,
Who, while they think they happiness enjoy,
Embrace a curse wrapt in delusive joy,
I reasoned thus—Since the Creator, God,
Who in eternal love has his abode,
Hath blended with the essence of the soul
An appetite, as fixed as the pole,
That's always eager in pursuit of bliss,
And always veering till it point to this,
There is some object adequate to fill
This boundless wish of our extended will.
Now, while my thought round nature's circle runs
(A bolder journey than the furious sun's)
This chief and satiating good to find,
The attracting centre of the human mind,
My ears they deafened, to my swimming eyes
His magic wand the drowsy god applies,
Bound all my senses in a silken sleep,
While mimic fancy did her vigils keep;
Yet still methinks some condescending power
Ranged the ideas in my mind that hour.

Methought I wandering was, with thousands more,
Beneath a high prodigious hill before,
Above the clouds whose towering summit rose,
With utmost labour only gained by those
Who grovelling prejudices threw away,
And with incessant straining climbed their way;
Where all who stood, their failing breath to gain,
With headlong ruin tumbled down amain.
This mountain is through every nation famed,
And, as I learned, Contemplation named.
O happy me! when I had reached its top
Unto my sight a boundless scene did ope.

First, sadly I surveyed with downward eye,
Of restless men below, the busy fry,
Who hunted trifles in an endless maze,
Like foolish boys on sunny summer days
Pursuing butterflies with all their might,
Who can't their troubles in the chase requite.
The painted insect he who most admires
Grieves most when it in his rude hand expires;
Or, should it live, with endless fears is tossed
Lest it take wing and be for ever lost.

Some men I saw their utmost art employ
How to attain a false deceitful joy,
Which from afar conspicuously did blaze,
And at a distance fixed their ravished gaze,
But nigh at hand it mocked their fond embrace;
When lo! again it flashed in their eyes,
But still, as they drew near, the fond illusion dies.
Just so I've seen a water-dog pursue
An unflown duck within his greedy view:
When he has, panting, at his prey arrived,
The coxcomb fooling—suddenly it dived;
He, gripping, is almost with water choked,
And grief, that all his towering hopes are mocked.
Then it emerges, he renews his toil,
And o'er and o'er again he gets the foil.
Yea, all the joys beneath the conscious sun,
And softer ones that his inspection shun,
Much of their pleasures in fruition fade;
Enjoyment o'er them throws a sullen shade.
The reason is, we promise vaster things
And sweeter joys than from their nature springs:
When they are lost, weep the apparent bliss,
And not what really in fruition is;
So that our griefs are greater than our joys,
And real pain springs from fantastic toys.

Though all terrene delights of men below
Are almost nothing but a glaring show;
Yet, if there always were a virgin joy,
When t'other fades, to soothe the wanton boy,
He somewhat might excuse his heedless course,
Some show of reason for the same enforce:
But frugal nature wisely does deny
To mankind such profuse variety;
Has only what is needful to us given,
To feed and cheer us in the way to Heaven;
And more would but the traveller delay,
Impede and clog him in his upward way.

I from the mount all mortal pleasures saw
Themselves within a narrow compass draw;
The libertine a nauseous circle run,
And dully acted what he'd often done.
Just so when Luna darts her silver ray,
And pours on silent earth a paler day;
From Stygian caves the flitting fairies scud,
And on the margent of some limpid flood,
Which by reflected moonlight darts a glance,

In midnight circles range themselves and dance.

To-morrow, cries he, will us entertain:
Pray what's to-morrow but to-day again?
Deluded youth, no more the chase pursue;
So oft deceived, no more the toil renew.
But in a constant and a fixed design
Of acting well there is a lasting mine
Of solid satisfaction, purest joy,
For virtue's pleasures never, never cloy:
Then hither come, climb up the steep ascent,
Your painful labour you will ne'er repent,
From Heaven itself here you're but one remove,
Here's the praeludium of the joys above,
Here you'll behold the awful Godhead shine,
And all perfections in the same combine;
You'll see that God, who, by his powerful call,
From empty nothing drew this spacious all,
Made beauteous order the rude mass control,
And every part subservient to the whole;
Here you'll behold upon the fatal tree
The God of nature bleed, expire, and die,
For such as 'gainst his holy laws rebel,
And such as bid defiance to his hell.
Through the dark gulf, here you may clearly pry
'Twixt narrow time and vast eternity;
Behold the Godhead, just as well as good,
And vengeance poured on tramplers on his blood;
But all the tears wiped from his people's eyes;
And, for their entrance, cleave the parting skies.
Then sure you will with holy ardours burn,
And to seraphic heats your passion turn;
Then in your eyes all mortal fair will fade,
And leave of mortal beauties but the shade;
Yourself to him you'll solemnly devote,
To him without whose providence you're not;
You'll of his service relish the delight,
And to his praises all your powers excite;
You'll celebrate his name in heavenly sound,
Which well-pleased skies in echoes will rebound:
This is the greatest happiness that can
Possessed be in this short life by man.

But darkly here the Godhead we survey,
Confined and cramped in this cage of clay.
What cruel band is this to earth that ties
Our souls from soaring to their native skies
Upon the bright eternal face to gaze,

And there drink in the beatific rays—
There to behold the good one and the fair,
A ray from whom all mortal beauties are?
In beauteous nature all the harmony
Is but the echo of the Deity,
Of all perfection who the centre is,
And boundless ocean of untainted bliss;
For ever open to the ravished view,
And full enjoyment of the radiant crew
Who live in raptures of eternal joy,
Whose flaming love their tuneful harps employ
In solemn hymns Jehovah's praise to sing,
And make all heaven with hallelujahs ring.

These realms of light no further I'll explore,
And in these heights I will no longer soar:
Not like our grosser atmosphere beneath,
The ether here's too thin for me to breathe.
The region is unsufferable bright,
And flashes on me with too strong a light.
Then from the mountain, lo! I now descend
And to my vision put a hasty end.

VERSES ON RECEIVING A FLOWER FROM A LADY

Madam, the flower that I received from you,
Ere I came home, had lost its lovely hue:
As flowers deprived of the genial day,
Its sprightly bloom did wither and decay:
Dear, fading flower, I know full well, said I,
The reason that you shed your sweets and die;
You want the influence of her enlivening eye.
Your case is mine: absence, that plague of love!
With heavy pace makes every minute move;
It of my being is an empty blank,
And hinders me myself with men to rank;
Your cheering presence quickens me again,
And new-sprung life exults in every vein.

ON BEAUTY

Beauty deserves the homage of the muse:
Shall mine, rebellious, the dear theme refuse?
No; while my breast respires the vital air,

Wholly I am devoted to the fair.
Beauty I'll sing in my sublimest lays,
I burn to give her just, immortal praise.
The heavenly maid with transport I'll pursue
To her abode, and all her graces view.

This happy place with all delights abounds,
And plenty broods upon the fertile grounds.
Here verdant grass their waving ???
And hills and vales in sweet confusion lie;
The nibbling flock stray o'er the rising hills,
And all around with bleating music fills;
High on their fronts tall blooming forests nod,
Of sylvan deities the blest abode;
The feathered minstrels hop from spray to spray,
And chant their gladsome carols all the day,
Till dusky night, advancing in her car,
Makes with declining light successful war.
Then Philomel her mournful lay repeats,
And through her throat breathes melancholy sweets.
Still higher yet wild rugged rocks arise,
That all ascent to human foot denies,
And strike beholders with a dread surprise.
This paradise these towering hills surround,
That thither is one only passage found.
Increasing brooks roll down the mountain's side,
And as they pass the opposing pebbles chide.

But vernal showers refresh the blooming year.
Their only season is eternal spring,
Which hovers o'er them with a downy wing;
Blossoms and fruits at once the trees adorn
With glowing blushes, like the rosy morn.

The way that to this stately palace goes
Of myrtle trees lies 'twixt two even rows,
Which, towering high, with outstretched arms displayed,
Over our heads a living arch have made.

To sing, my muse, the bold attempt begin,
Of awful beauties you behold within:
The Goddess sat upon a throne of gold,
Embossed with figures charming to behold;
Here new-made Eve stood in her early bloom,
Not yet obscured with sin's sullen gloom;
Her naked beauties do the soul confound,
From every part is given a fatal wound;
There other beauties of a meaner fame

Oblige the sight, whom here I shall not name.
In her right hand she did a sceptre sway
O'er all mankind, ambitious to obey: so
Her lovely forehead and her killing eye,
Her blushing cheeks of a vermilion dye,
Her lip's soft pulp, her heaving snowy breast,
Her well-turned arm, her handsome slender waist,
And all below veiled from the curious eye—
Oh! heavenly maid! makes all beholders cry.

Her dress was plain, not pompous as a bride,
Which would her sweeter native beauties hide.
One thing I mind, a spreading hoop she wore,
Than which no thing adorns a lady more.
With equal rage could I its beauties sing,
I'd with the hoop make all Parnassus ring.
Around her shoulders, dangling on her throne,
A bright Tartana carelessly was thrown,
Which has already won immortal praise,
Most sweetly sung in Allan Ramsay's lays;
The wanton Cupids did around her play,
And smiling loves upon her bosom stray;
With purple wings they round about her flew,
And her sweet lips tinged with ambrosial dew.

Her air was easy, graceful was her mien,
Her presence banished the ungrateful spleen;
In short, her divine influence refined
Our corrupt hearts, and polished mankind.

Of lovely nymphs she had a smiling train,
Fairer than those e'er graced Arcadia's plain.
The British ladies next to her took place,
Who chiefly did the fair assembly grace.
What blooming virgins can Britannia boast,
Their praises would all eloquence exhaust.
With ladies there my ravished eyes did meet
That oft I've seen grace fair Edina's street,
With their broad hoops cut through the willing air,
Pleased to give place unto the lovely fair:

Sure this is like those blissful seats above;
[For] here is peace, transporting joy, and love.

Should I be doomed by cruel angry fate
In some lone isle my lingering end to wait,
Yet happy I! still happy should I be!
While blest with virtue and a charming she;

With full content I'd fortune's pride despise,
And die still gazing on her lovely eyes.

May all the blessings mortals need below,
May all the blessings heaven can bestow,
May every thing that's pleasant, good, or rare,
Be the eternal portion of the fair.

A PASTORAL ENTERTAINMENT

While in heroic numbers some relate
The amazing turns of wise eternal fate,
Exploits of heroes in the dusty field,
That to their name immortal honour yield;
Grant me, ye powers, fast by the limpid spring
The harmless revels of the plain to sing.
At a rich feast, kept each revolving year,
Their fleecy care when joyful shepherds shear,
A wreath of flowers culled from the neighbouring lands
Is all the prize my humble muse demands.

Now blithesome shepherds, by the early dawn,
Their new-shorn flocks drive to the dewy lawn;
While, in a bleating language, each salutes
The welcome morning and their fellow brutes:
Then all prepared for the rural feast,
And in their finest Sunday habits drest;
The crystal brook supplied the mirror's place,
[Wherein] they bathed and viewed their cleanly face,
[Then swains] and nymphs resorted to the fields
[Adorned with all the] pomp the country yields.

The place appointed was a spacious vale,
Fanned always by a cooling western gale,
Which in soft breezes through the meadows stray,
And steals the ripened fragrances away;
With native incense all the air perfumes,
Renewing with its genial breath the blooms.
Here every shepherd might his flocks survey,
Securely roam and take his harmless play;
And here were flowers each shepherdess to grace,
On her fair bosom courting but a place.

Now in this vale, beneath a grateful shade,
By twining boughs of spreading beeches made,
On seats of homely turf themselves they placed,

And cheerfully enjoyed their rural feast,
Consisting of the product of the fields,
And all the luxury the country yields.

No maddening liquors spoiled their harmless mirth;
But an untainted spring their thirst allayed,
Which in meanders through the valley strayed.
Thrice happy swains! who spend your golden days
In country pastime, and, when night displays
Her sable shade, to peaceful huts retire;
Can any man a sweeter bliss desire?
In ancient times so passed the smiling hour,
When our first parents lived in Eden's bower,
Ere care and trouble were pronounced our doom,
Or sin had blasted the creation's bloom.

AN ELEGY UPON JAMES THERBURN IN CHATTO

Now, Chatto, you're a dreary place—
Pale sorrow broods on ilka face
Therburn has run his . . race,

And now, and now, ah me, alace!
The carle lies dead.
Having his paternoster said,
He took a dram and went to bed;
He fell asleep, and death was glad
That he did catch him;
For Therburn was e'en ill-bested,
That none did watch him.
For had the carle but been aware,
That meagre death, who none does spare,
T'attempt sic things should ever dare,
As stop his pipe;
He might have come to flee or skare
The greedy gipe.
Now had he but a gill or twae
Death wou'd nae got the victory sae,
Nor put poor Therburn o'er the brae,
Into the grave;
The fumbling fellow, some folks say,
Should be jobbed on baith night and day;
She had without'en better play
Remained still
Barren for ever and for aye,
Do what he will.

Therefore they say he got some help
In getting of the little whelp;
But passing that, it makes me yelp,
But what remead?
Death lent him sic a cursed skelp,
That now he's dead.
Therburn, for evermore farewell,
And be thy grave baith dry and deep;
And rest thy carcass soft and well,
Free from
no night
Disturb

ON THE HOOP

The hoop, the darling justly of the fair,
Of every generous swain deserves the care.
It is unmanly to desert the weak,
'Twould urge a stone, if possible to speak;
To hear stanch hypocrites bawl out, and cry,
'This hoop's a whorish garb, fie! ladies, fie!'
O cruel and audacious men, to blast
The fame of ladies, more than vestals chaste;
Should you go search the globe throughout,
You will find none so pious and devout;
So modest, chaste, so handsome, and so fair,
As our dear Caledonian ladies are.
When awful beauty puts on all her charms,
Nought gives our sex such terrible alarms,
As when the hoop and tartan both combine
To make a virgin like a goddess shine.
Let quakers cut their clothes unto the quick,
And with severities themselves afflict;
But may the hoop adorn Edina's street,
Till the south pole shall with the northern meet!

AN ELEGY ON PARTING

It was a sad, ay, 'twas a sad farewell,
I still afresh the pangs of parting feel.
Against my breast my heart impatient beat,
And in deep sighs bemoaned its cruel fate
Thus with the object of my love to part,
My life! my joy! 'twould rend a rocky heart.

Where'er I turn myself, where'er I go,
I meet the image of my lovely foe;
With witching charms the phantom still appears,
And with her wanton smiles insults my tears;
Still haunts the places where we used to walk,
And where with raptures oft I heard her talk:
Those scenes I now with deepest sorrow view,
And sighing bid to all delight adieu.

While I my head upon this turf recline,
Officious sun, in vain on me you shine;
In vain unto the smiling fields I hie;
In vain the flowery meads salute my eye;
In vain the cheerful birds and shepherds sing,
And with their carols make the valleys ring;
Yea, all the pleasure that the country yield
Can't me from sorrow for her absence shield:
With divine pleasure books which one inspire,
Yea, books themselves I do not now admire.
But hark! methinks some pitying power I hear,
This welcome message whisper in my ear:
'Forget thy groundless griefs, dejected swain—
You and the nymph you love shall meet again;
No more your muse shall sing such mournful lays,
But bounteous heaven and your kind mistress praise.'

THE MONTH OF MAY

Among the changing months May stands confest
The sweetest, and in fairest colours drest;
Soft as the breeze that fans the smiling field,
Sweet as the breath that opening roses yield,
Fair as the colour lavish nature paints
On virgin flowers free from unodorous taints.
To rural scenes thou tempt'st the busy crowd,
Who in each grove thy praises sing aloud.
The blooming belles and shallow beaux, strange sight!
Turn nymphs and swains, and in their sports delight.

MORNING IN THE COUNTRY

When from the opening chambers of the east
The morning springs, in thousand liveries drest,

The early larks their morning tribute pay,
And in shrill notes salute the blooming day.
Refreshed fields with pearly dew do shine,
And tender blades therewith their tops incline.
Their painted leaves the unblown flowers expand,
And with their odorous breath perfume the land.
The crowing cock and clattering hen awakes
Dull sleepy clowns, who know the morning breaks.
The herd his plaid around his shoulders throws,
Grasps his dear crook, calls on his dog, and goes;
Around the fold he walks with careful pace,
And fallen clods sets in their wonted place;
Then opes the door, unfolds his fleecy care,
And gladly sees them crop their morning fare!
Down upon easy moss his limbs he lays,
And sings some charming shepherdess's praise.

LISY'S PARTING WITH HER CAT

The dreadful hour with leaden pace approached,
Lashed fiercely on by unrelenting fate,
When Lisy and her bosom Cat must part:
For now, to school and pensive needle doomed,
She's banished from her childhood's undashed joy,
And all the pleasing intercourse she kept
With her gray comrade, which has often soothed
Her tender moments, while the world around
Glowed with ambition, business, and vice,
Or lay dissolved in sleep's delicious arms;
And from their dewy orbs the conscious stars
Shed on their friendship influence benign.
But see where mournful Puss, advancing, stood
With outstretched tail, casts looks of anxious woe
On melting Lisy, in whose eye the tear
Stood tremulous, and thus would fain have said,
If nature had not tied her struggling tongue:
'Unkind, O! who shall now with fattening milk,
With flesh, with bread, and fish beloved, and meat,
Regale my. taste? and at the cheerful fire,
Ah, who shall bask me in their downy lap?
Who shall invite me to the bed, and throw
The bedclothes o'er me in the winter night,
When Eurus roars? Beneath whose soothing hand
Soft shall I purr? But now, when Lisy's gone,
What is the dull officious world to me?
I loathe the thoughts of life:' Thus plained the Cat,

While Lisy felt, by sympathetic touch,
These anxious thoughts that in her mind revolved,
And casting on her a desponding look,
She snatched her in her arms with eager grief,
And mewing, thus began:—' O Cat beloved!
Thou dear companion of my tender years!
Joy of my youth! that oft hast licked my hands
With velvet tongue ne'er stained by mouse's blood.
Oh, gentle Cat! how shall I part with thee?
How dead and heavy will the moments pass
When you are not in my delighted eye,
With Cubi playing, or your flying tail.
How harshly will the softest muslin feel,
And all the silk of schools, while I no more
Have your sleek skin to soothe my softened sense?
How shall I eat while you are not beside
To share the bit? How shall I ever sleep
While I no more your lulling murmurs hear?
Yet we must part—so rigid fate decrees—
But never shall your loved idea dear
Part from my soul, and when I first can mark
The embroidered figure on the snowy lawn,
Your image shall my needle keen employ.
Hark! Now I'm called away! O direful sound!
I come—I come, but first I charge you all—
You—you—and you, particularly you,
O, Mary, Mary, feed her with the best,
Repose her nightly in the warmest couch,
And be a Lisy to her! '—Having said,
She set her down, and with her head across,
Rushed to the evil which she could not shun,
While a sad mew went knelling to her heart!

LINES ON MARLEFIELD

The seat of Sir William Bennet, of Grubbat, Bart.

What is the task that to the muse belongs?
What but to deck in her harmonious songs
The beauteous works of nature and of art,
Rural retreats that cheer the heavy heart?
Then Marlefield begin, my muse, and sing;
With Marlefield the hills and vales shall ring.
O! what delight and pleasure 'tis to rove
Through all the walks and alleys of this grove,
Where spreading trees a checkered scene display,

Partly admitting and excluding day;
Where cheerful green and odorous sweets conspire
The drooping soul with pleasure to inspire;
Where little birds employ their narrow throats
To sing its praises in unlaboured notes.
To it adjoined a rising fabric stands,
Which with its state our silent awe commands.
Its endless beauties mock the poet's pen;
So to the garden I'll return again.
Pomona makes the trees with fruit abound,
And blushing Flora paints the enamelled ground.
Here lavish nature does her stores disclose,
Flowers of all hue, their queen the bashful rose;
With their sweet breath the ambient air's perfumed,
Nor is thereby their fragrant stores consumed;
O'er the fair landscape sportive zephyrs scud,
And by kind force display the infant bud.
The vegetable kind here rear their head,
By kindly showers and heaven's indulgence fed:
Of fabled nymphs such were the sacred haunts,
But real nymphs this charming dwelling vaunts.
Now to the greenhouse let's awhile retire,
To shun the heat of Sol's infectious fire:
Immortal authors grace this cool retreat,
Of ancient times and of a modern date.
Here would my praises and my fancy dwell;
But it, alas, description does excel.
O may this sweet, this beautiful abode
Remain the charge of the eternal God.

A POETICAL EPISTLE TO SIR WILLIAM BENNET

Written in 1714, aet. 14

My trembling muse your honour does address.
That it's a bold attempt most humbly I confess.
If you'll encourage her young fagging flight,
She'll upwards soar and mount Parnassus' height.
If little things with great may be compared,
In Rome it so with the divine Virgil fared;
The tuneful bard Augustus did inspire
Made his great genius flash poetic fire;
But, if upon my flight your honour frowns,
The muse folds up her wings, and, dying, justice owns.

TO ELUCIDATE AND ILLUSTRATE THE LIFE AND TIMES OF JAMES THOMSON

1666. Birth of Thomas Thomson, the poet's father. Minister of Ednam, Roxburghshire. 1693. Marries Beatrix, daughter of Alexander Trotter, of Widehope (a small lairdship in Roxburghshire).

1694. Birth of Voltaire.

1700. Birth, at Ednam or Widehope, of James Thomson, the poet—fourth child (third son) of his parents; born (probably) on the 7th, baptized on the 15th of September. In the November following, his father inducted into the parish of Southdean, Roxburghshire. Birth of David Malloch (or Mallet). Death of Dryden.

1709. Birth of Johnson. 1712. Young Thomson attends a Grammar School in Jedburgh, some eight miles or so from Southdean. His acquaintance with Mr. (afterwards the Rev.) Robert Riccaltoun, farmer at Earlshaugh, begins about this time. First attempts at versifying, a year or two later.

1715. Young Thomson enters Edinburgh University.

1716. Death of his father, in February, while exorcizing a ghost. Home transferred to Edinburgh.

1719. Death of Addison.

1720. Thomson now a student of Divinity. Continues versifying, chiefly on rural subjects in the heroic couplet; contributes to The Edinburgh Miscellany Of a Country Life, &c.

1721. Birth of Collins. Walpole Prime Minister (till 1742).

1724. Thomson still at the University. Adverse criticism, by the Professor of Divinity, of one of his college exercises (a discourse on the 10th portion of Psalm cxix), the turning-point of his life.

1725. End of February, Thomson sets out to seek his fortune in London: embarks at Leith, not again to see Scotland. Visits Drury Lane Theatre, and sees Gato acted. Death of his mother, in May. In July, acting as tutor to Lord Binning's son, at Barnet, near London. Composition of Winter in the following autumn and winter. Publication of Allan Ramsay's The Gentle Shepherd.

1726. I March, Winter, a thin folio of 16 pp., 40511., price 18., John Millan, publisher. Dyer's Grongar Hill published. Thomson acting as tutor in an academy in London. Acquaintance with Aaron Hill. Second edition of Winter, in June.

1727. Death of Sir Isaac Newton: in June, Thomson publishes a poem To the Memory of Newton. Summer published; a second edition the same year. Thomson now relying on literature for his support. Britannia written (not published till 1729), in opposition to the peace-at-any-price policy of Walpole. The poet spends part of the summer at Marlborough Castle (the guest of the Countess of Hertford).

1728. Spring published by Andrew Millar. Goldsmith born.

1729. Death of Congreve: anonymous poem To the Memory of Congreve published; attributed to Thomson on very unsatisfactory evidence. In September, Thomson the guest of Bubb Dodington at Eastbury. The poet busy in various ways—with the tragedy of Sophonisba, the completion of The Seasons, the publication of Britannia, and contributions to Ralph's, Miscellany; among the last a Hymn, on Solitude, The Happy Man, and a metrical version of a passage of St. Matthew's Gospel.

1730. Publication of the first collected edition of The Seasons (including Autumn and the Hymn for the first time): two editions, one in quarto at a guinea, published by subscription; the other in octavo. Sophonisba produced at Drury Lane, February 28th, Mrs. Oldfield taking the part of the heroine: a success on the stage, despite one weak line, and selling well when printed. Travelling tutor to young Charles Talbot, son of Mr. Charles Talbot, then Solicitor-General (soon afterwards Lord Chancellor); in Paris in December, where (probably) he visits Voltaire.

1731. Visits most of the courts and capital cities of Europe (Murdoch); in Paris in October. Visits Italy—'I long to see the fields where Virgil gathered his immortal honey,' &c. Collecting material for his poem on Liberty. Correspondence with Dodington—' Should you inquire after my muse, I believe she did not cross the Channel with me.' Probably wrote, however, the lines on the death of Aikman, the painter. Returns to England in December. Birth of Cowper. The Gentleman's Magazine established.

1733. Death of young Talbot in September; the elder becomes Lord Chancellor in November; soon after, Thomson appointed Secretary of Briefs in the Court of Chancery—the post a sinecure with about 300l. a year. Some personal stanzas of The Castle of Indolence written about this time.

1735. Publication of Liberty; Parts I, II, and III, at intervals.

1736. Liberty, Parts IV and V at intervals. Thomson goes to live in Kew Lane, Richmond—his residence for the rest of his life. Intimacy with Pope, whose house was only a mile off, at Twickenham. Busy with the drama—'whipping and spurring to finish a tragedy this winter.' Sends pecuniary assistance to his sisters in Edinburgh. Becomes acquainted with 'Amanda'.

1737. Death of Lord Chancellor Talbot, in February; Thomson's memorial verses (panegyric and elegy) in June. Writing Agamemnon. Loss of Secretaryship. Acquaintance with George Lyttelton. Pension of 100l. a year from the Prince of Wales, to whom Liberty had been dedicated. Shenstone's Schoolmistress published.

1738. Thomson's Preface to Milton's Areopagitica appears. Agamemnon produced in April, Quin in the title role. A new edition (a reprint of octavo edition of 1730) of The Seasons brought out.

1739. Thomson's tragedy of Edward and Eleonora prohibited by the censorship.

1740. Conjointly with Malloch, The Masque of Alfred, containing the ode 'Rule, Britannia', performed August 1, in Clifden Gardens, before the Prince of Wales. 1742. Young's Night thoughts (Books I-III). 1743. Visits the Lytteltons, at Hagley Park, in August—'I am come to the most agreeable place and company in the world.' Correspondence with 'Amanda'.—' But wherever I am... I never cease to think of my loveliest Miss Young. You are part of my being; you mix with all my thoughts.' His song, For ever, Fortune, wilt thou prove, ' about this time. Preparing, at Hagley, a revised edition of The Seasons with Lyttelton's assistance.

1744. New edition of The Seasons, with many alterations and additions. Lyttelton in office: he appoints Thomson Surveyor-General of the Leeward Islands—a sinecure post, worth 300l. a year clear. Death of Pope.

1745. His best drama Tancred and Sigismunda produced at Drury Lane, with Garrick as Tancred. At Hagley in the summer.

1746. Thomson makes way for his friend (and deputy), William Paterson, in the office of Surveyor-General. At Hagley in the autumn. Last edition of The Seasons published in the poet's lifetime. Collins's Odes published.

1747. At Hagley in the autumn. Visits Shenstone at the Leasowes. Busy at Coriolanus (nearly finished in March).

1748. Prince of Wales's displeasure with Lyttelton visited on Lyttelton's friends—Thomson's name struck off pension list. The Castle of Indolence, in May. Death of Thomson, after short illness, at Richmond, August 27th. Buried in Richmond churchyard. Collins's Ode in memory of Thomson—a lasting memorial.

1749. Coriolanus produced, in January—the Prologue by Lyttelton.

1753. Shiels's Life of Thomson (Cibber's Life of the Poets)

1758. Death of Allan Ramsay.

1759. Birth of Burns.

1762. Murdoch's Memoir of Thomson (prefixed to an edition of Thomson's Works). Monument to Thomson in Westminster Abbey.

1781. Johnson's Life of Thomson (Lives of the Poets).

1791. Burns's Address to the Shade of Thomson.

1792. The Earl of Buchan's Essay on the Life of the Poet Thomson

1831. Biography of Thomson by Sir Harris Nicholas (prefixed to the Aldine Edition of Thomson's Works: annotated by P, Cunningham, 1860).

1842. An edition of The Seasons, with notes by Bolton Corney.

1891. Clarendon Press edition of The Seasons and The Castle of Indolence, with a biographical notice and full notes by J. Logie Robertson.

1894. Furth in Field (Part IV—On the poet of The Seasons), by Hugh Haliburton.

1895. James Thomson: Sa Vie et ses Oeuvres (678 pp.), by Leon Morel.

1898. James Thomson (in Famous Scots Series), by W. Bayne.

1908. James Thomson (in English Men of Letters Series), by G. C. Macaulay.

www.ingramcontent.com/pod-product-compliance
Lightning Source LLC
Chambersburg PA
CBHW021940040426
42448CB00008B/1157